BITTERSWEET

A Memoir

BITTER SWEET

The Life and Times of the World's Leading Chocolate Taster

A Memoir

ANGUS KENNEDY

APOLLO
PUBLISHERS

BITTERSWEET

THE LIFE AND TIMES OF THE WORLD'S LEADING CHOCOLATE TASTER

Apollo Publishers books may be purchased for educational, business, or sales promotional use. Special editions may be made available upon request. For details, contact Apollo Publishers at info@apollopublishers.com.

Visit our website at www.apollopublishers.

Library of Congress Cataloging-in-Publication Data is available on file.

Cover design by Rain Saukas.

Print ISBN: 978-1-948062-04-6

Ebook ISBN: 978-1-948062-11-4

Printed in the United States of America.

CONTENTS

PREFACE

Okay, I'm not into long lists of thank-yous extended to people neither of us would care to meet.

However, there is one person I should mention: the anesthetist who yesterday put me to sleep for an operation to remove a cyst on my left knee. Yes, he deserves to be on my list of honors. Wow, those anesthetics are amazing. I mean, what is that drug they give you before the one that makes you sleep? You know, the one that says, *Hey, Angus, it doesn't matter if they chop off your entire leg or if chocolate runs out forever—nothing matters!*

Just looking into the anesthetist's face, fully equipped with one dark eyebrow with the curious ability to move on its own, while the other, a light-colored one, remained stationary, was a good start. Watching this facial performance while he proceeded to proudly name all the drugs he was administering as my consciousness drifted into the ether: now that was pretty damned cool.

Angus Kennedy you're going down.

It was a general anesthetic of course, and I fell asleep the moment I started to lie back and felt the nurse's hands guide my head. The operation was, I say, almost a success. They found not one, but three "foreign bodies," which they presented to me in a small blue pot when I woke up (now sent off for analysis), floating around the soft tissues at the back of my knee. Four years of pain are now almost over.

I think I am high from yesterday's drugs. I must be, and because of that and not being able to stand up, I am here now finishing this book on the couch with a single origin bar of French chocolate handy. (That is also keeping me on the couch!) So we should all thank him, and chocolate of course, and not a boring list of lifeless aunties and distant acquaintances.

I'm a man with five kids, an impossibly busy job in confectionery conferencing and magazines, and never enough time even to escape to the bathroom in the mornings before I have to perform the most intolerable school runs ever in a ten-year-old Land Cruiser. So how was I ever going write a book—another book, even, I asked myself? But once I started, I knew it would be okay. You can't leave off books when you write them. They're like plants; they need feeding or they die.

So now I am back home, sitting in the living room over the school holidays with my knee up and trying (rather foolishly) to concentrate with an Xbox on in the background and three overactive boys shooting anything they see on the screen. At last I have the chance—the book I have been meaning to finish *will* be finished, thanks to my wife, Sophie, now with a drugged-up cripple on the couch during Easter, who at every juncture is being asked, "What can I do now, Mum? I'm bored."

Ah, Easter: a period in which we in the United Kingdom spend about £2,462 million on chocolate, which translates into 70,000 tons of it, according to the International Cocoa Organization. Not much when the world munches through 7.6 million tons a year. Yes, a celebration during which British kids, on average, consume 8.8 chocolate eggs each; each egg averages about 750 calories. That's 6,600 calories, enough for each child to run from London to Oxford without stopping.

So I confess: my world—and the act of feeding my family—rely on chocolate. I have made a living out of "loving" a product that can rot your teeth, make you fat, take control, and see us all coming helplessly back for more. It's time not just for me to make a few personal confessions, but at last, it's confession time for the whole industry. And my first confession is one of the most difficult for many to swallow.

INTRODUCTION

Welcome to my job. I confess: I get paid to eat and write about chocolate and candy each and every day that I am still alive. *The* best job ever, some say.

And welcome to my world: chocolate, a substance that contains nearly the highest calorie content of any food and is one of the most addictive, too. A hefty 90 percent of American citizens vote it as their favorite flavor, while according to recent research by Fererro, 43 percent of Brits would give up booze for it, 35 percent religion, 27 percent would never wear their favorite pair of shoes again, and 9 percent admit they would give up sex for chocolate.

So, the basic truth is that I fly around the world visiting chocolate factories and sampling their confections directly from conveyor belts for my articles and various media assignments. When I am not in factories eating these goodies, extra chocolates and candies are delivered almost daily onto my office desk with ever more creative deliveries. That's nuts, right?

I even have a chocolate coffee table in my office. It was presented to me as a gift after a global chocolate convention. It's mostly eaten now, mainly because I enjoy the occasional snap as I break off pieces and consume my table in front of my guests. Chocolate sculpture is a big thing now, especially in Paris, where the competitions last for days on end. You can hardly tell these things are made out of chocolate; they make anything from shoes to famous faces to entire landscapes, detailed with edible spray paint. It's all a bit ridiculous if you really think about it.

There are people out there who love chocolate far more than I do and deserve to have it more than I do. But life isn't like that. Anyone who believes life is fair is very lucky.

I didn't plan or really deserve the dream job of being Britain's chief chocolate taster. But it seems to *have to be* this way. Besides, we don't apply for the best jobs in the world, we *create* them. We always create the most enjoyable things. We never seem to work for them. How can anything be enjoyable if we have to work for it anyway?

Journalists and television presenters with jobs that I would die for say to me, "Angus, I want your job." We go into the TV studio (where I hand out chocolates, of course) and it goes like this: "Now, let's go over to meet our next guest, Angus Kennedy. Yes, we have the world's expert on chocolate here in the studio, who is, wait for it . . . paid to eat chocolates. I want his job."

And I'm thinking, as I am being interviewed and almost revered (even more ridiculous), "Well, yes, I *do* eat chocolate for a living, but I also do lots of *other* things as well. I run a small publishing business, I edit, I write articles, I sell books, I take kids to school, I empty the dishwasher, I try to fix broken lawn mowers, and I attempt to mend things that I can't mend just because I am called 'Dad.'" They don't see the other bits, like me trying to maintain my weight with a bad knee and having to get all my teeth capped in advance at huge expense due to the large number of sweets I *have* to eat.

But they're having none of it. They have a real Willy Wonka who is paid to eat chocolate, and that's enough; nothing else matters. So, meet Angus Kennedy, the British eccentric who does absolutely nothing else at all but fly around the world gulping copious amounts of delish confections.

We have to dream—it's good to dream. Life is made possible by dreams. Perhaps we want to believe that we can eat candy all the time and be paid for the pleasure. Dreams deserve to be where they belong, realized before we die.

Well, I thought, if so many people want this "dream job," which I do in part have, then of course I will write a book about it and how I landed it, and show you what it's like in a secret industry about which so little is known. Oh, and I will address the question "Will we run out of chocolate?"

I did seem to achieve the impossible, so I am going to tell you about how I became a Willy Wonka. I failed my way to success! Sometimes you don't really have to work that hard to succeed. We make it easy to make life difficult, but make it difficult to make life easy.

In fact, the harder you chase your goals, the more likely it is that they will run deeper into the forest. And, most likely, what we *are* chasing is something that we never were supposed to catch anyway. We keep hunting, never catch anything, and die pursuing something that was never supposed to be for us. Luckily, I failed a lot.

And then I made it at fifty-two years old, going gray, relying on my five kids' memories, and having to ask my wife to speak a little louder and read the menu for me at the local French restaurant in Kent when we go out, because (again) I forgot my reading glasses and it's too dark.

If I can make it at fifty-plus and change my career against all odds, with everything I have been through, then come on—you can do it, too. We can achieve anything in five years. I am here for no other purpose than to inspire you to be the great person that lies within you, the person you were all along.

I do keep failing. But the only real failure is to not get up again. *It's not about how you are knocked down, it's about getting up—time after time.*

So here I am, for better or for worse, at your service. Was this absurd job my planning? Will I be a chocolate Wonka of tomorrow? Who cares? I don't know, but I embrace whatever happens as long as *something* happens. Success is being you as you travel through the changes.

My story is about how I landed the best job in the world despite the worst preparation possible. We all seem to worry about what we don't have as opposed to thinking about how great it is to have what we do.

There is a magical space beyond what we can dream. For some of us, great success happens, and for others it simply doesn't. But those who succeed are able to travel beyond their dreams without fear. I'm still trying, but no one goes anywhere by doing nothing and fearing change. You have to get up again, and again, and again. And then discover what the actual real dream holds for you.

So let's get on with the important stuff, namely my entry into the world of candy and how I became a chief chocolate taster, got the best job in the world, and became a TV personality by failing at everything and finally accepting and letting go. Here's how I mysteriously seemed to get ahead with the worst preparation and entered the secret doors to the Kingdom of Chocolate. Here's to always expecting the unexpected—the only thing we can ever truly expect.

Jump into the time machine and get comfy, it's time for liftoff. I'm going to take you back to 1973, to my extremely unpredictable family house in Muswell Hill, North London (a story in itself), where the candy-crazed kid was in the making.

CHAPTER 1

Mad Dogs, Vodka, and Candy

MUSWELL HILL, NORTH LONDON, 1973

I never saw much of our mail as a child, as most of it was ripped up by our overexcited dogs, deranged rescue cases from a 1970s Battersea dog shelter. As soon as the tip of a letter made itself visible through the letterbox, these hopelessly untrained hounds would come cascading down the stairs in search of their morning snack and collapse in a heap, waiting for the mail to drop conveniently into their mouths. It was a race between me and the dogs to get to the door. There was good reason I was keen on beating them to it.

My mother was probably sleeping over her desk in her home office on the ground floor, holding an empty vodka bottle concealed in a paper bag. (I didn't need to look; I just knew.) With my father—who was, unbeknownst to me, in the very late stages of cancer—bedridden, she had given up completely.

Booze was her new master, and at nine years old, mine was fast becoming candy. It was my job to rescue the candy and checks in the mail, or the mortgage wouldn't get paid. I was unaware that our mortgage was heavily in arrears and I didn't know that not all households were like mine, but I had a feeling that things were not right.

In essence, I should not be the world's leading chocolate taster today; I should be on the scrap heap!

Despite the somewhat uncomfortable combination of candy, cancer, and empty spirit bottles badly hidden around the house, it wasn't until later in life that I realized my childhood home was not normal by any standards at all. It was, however, a brilliant place for learning about life and the confectionery industry. At the time, I ate candy to *keep* living; nowadays I eat it *for* a living. I am still dependent on the stuff today.

The Kennedys' unlikely candy school took place in our Edwardian family house in Muswell Hill, North London. The dogs—Peggy and Sheba—and I ate the sweets, my mum knocked back the vodka, and my dad struggled with the malignant tumor feeding off him.

Oh, and the banks didn't want to be left out either, so they were swarming like wasps for their fix of what seemed to be an imminent repossession. It was a magnificent cocktail of catastrophe, high sugar intake, alcohol consumption, and my disastrous education.

Candy samples from confectioners around the world arrived regularly through the letterbox, and both the wretched animals and I couldn't wait to see what goodies were in store. We were all hungry. The free samples were from companies that wanted my mother to write about them. I was keen to beat the dogs to the door, as the mail contained what was often my breakfast too.

My mother, when she eventually woke up from her naps on the desk, wrote about these new-to-market confections for the family confectionery magazine, which today is called *Kennedy's Confection*. The journal, of which I am now editor, is one of the oldest business journals in the world; it even survived two world wars. Though the original name was *Confectionery News* in 1890, it has only changed names twice in 125 years. At this time, during the 1970s, it was called *Confectionery Manufacture and Marketing*, which was a mouthful for our customers, most of whom were learning English as a foreign language, so I changed it to its current title, *Kennedy's Confection*, in 1990.

The family company was started by my father, John Kennedy, and my mother, who used the pen name Margaret Lang, who together acquired the magazine in 1971, along with many other magazine titles, including a turkey industry magazine, an ice-cream magazine, and something called *Chemistry and Industry Buyer's Guide*, which I never even tried to understand because I always used to think it was *the* most boring magazine ever printed.

Today, many of the dog-eared issues are in my cellar, sitting in suitcases and cartons, or in a dark corner of my attic slowly being forgotten about over time. I am the only person now alive who knows where they are. Sometimes I take a step back in time and go up to the loft (which incidentally was built in 1860 so adds to the effect nicely), sit on an old oak beam, and tune into the past.

Sweets tended to be defined by their shapes one hundred years ago, and many products mentioned in the magazines in my attic are now all but forgotten, with product names like Marzipan Sweets, Acid Drops, Fairy Rock, Twisted Barley Sugars, Silver Comfits, and my favorite, Voice Pellets. Quite what they did for your voice, I still don't know. Perhaps they provided the energy to shout louder for more drops.

Even the currency was better back then. Buying anything was far more engaging than it is today. The money had character and influence on your feelings; we could go into a sweetshop on the corner with a half farthing, a shilling, a crown, or guinea in our pocket. How romantic shopping for sweets used to be with words like that! Now it's a mere mundane mechanical swipe of our debit card over a machine as both customer and seller fail to look at each other, register any appropriate human engagement, or smile.

Yes, shopping for sweets, though rewarding, is now just a monotonous beep in a supermarket as we watch them move along the conveyor belt, as we feel guilty and wonder if behind their wry smiles the checkout staff are really thinking we are just plain English Saddleback pigs. It's nothing like walking along the beech-tree–lined country lane to the village shop with your last farthing and wondering with every step what dreams it could buy; perhaps I am far too romantic.

My mother was the editor then, and she also sold advertising space, which is a tough job, especially with a dying husband in the background. Over time my father's illness took its hold, and with my mother's drinking, only one magazine made it through to today—the confectionery magazine.

So, the sweets arrived in the mail and I would dig in right away and my mother would come into the lounge, before taking another secret swig of her bottle, and ask me what the sweets tasted like. I would say, "Yeah, great, Mum, sweet." She would nod in approval, return to her desk, push her greasy glasses back to the top of her nose, and hit the keys of her self-correcting IBM Selectric golf ball typewriter. For the rest of the day, in between sleeping and sipping from a bottle wrapped in an old Budgens supermarket paper bag, she proceeded—God knows how—to write an issue of the confectionery magazine for that month.

The magazine had great authority. Oddly, my mother was a very good writer and wonderful with people. She managed to hide the drinking problem (with my help) in the beginning. Perhaps it was all that booze that gave her such a wild imagination.

Sometimes, though, I craved a conversation with a normal mum. I used to think a lot about life, and I would often sit alone on the grassy bank beside the school playground while my friends played football.

I never really found anyone to fill the gap until my mother finally married again, so for the time being I learned to reason for myself, which became a huge asset and in some ways taught me to be spiritual, as I would find myself talking to an imaginary guardian angel, something I still do to this day.

I would watch the other kids kick the ball from left to right and get upset at random moments when they didn't have the ball and duly found myself looking for reason for my place in the world, if it wasn't shouting about the placement of a ball. When I took a good look inside, I felt that I was just as freaky as my mother.

There was life in between my family's nourishment of confectionery, booze, and nearer-to-death-every-day experiences. In a way, perhaps, both Mum and I were addicted and needed our regular fixes. I didn't know any other way. There always was and always would be endless amounts of chocolate, toffees, bubble gum, and whatever I wanted, just about whenever I wanted to eat it. But free candy for a schoolkid was an eyebrow-raising thing to have on tap no matter what was happening at home.

In those days, you could eat as you wished and not be in the slightest bit concerned about *what* you ate. We didn't worry about choosing fair trade, UTZ certified coffee beans, or Rainforest Alliance–approved chocolates, for example. We didn't feel guilty if we chose our food from non-sustainable sources or from children trafficked into the trade in Western Africa. And we didn't worry about the nutritional content. We didn't know any better.

Our confectionery in the 1970s was packed full of artificial colors and flavors, but we didn't mind. We quite happily got on with the important task of destroying the planet. Nowadays, we're bombarded with new, often conflicting takes on why we should or should not eat something. But in those days, we did as we wanted and didn't care too much that 80 percent of our confectionery contained artificial colors. (Now 85 percent doesn't.)

For better or for worse, my childhood diet was brilliantly inappropriate. I certainly wasn't on the receiving end of good nutritional advice. It didn't seem to make a huge difference eating all that lot then. Despite my dreadful diet in my youth, I went on to row for England for the Under 23's British junior team in 1986 in a coxless pair, and that was just before winning Henley Royal Regatta in a coxed four, a few years later.

Here I am today as one of the leading experts on candy and sugar consumption.

But now at least I can say I know how bad the things that I am eating are, when previously I had no idea.

My diet was a hit-or-miss affair. Breakfast, for example, was cooked in a frying pan that was seldom washed up, so fried eggs would have these disgusting lumps of burned garlic embedded into the base of the new, crispy, overcooked fried eggs that went into the pan.

I was overweight and my teeth were desperately out of line and full of gaping holes. I did have some dental treatment when my mother remembered, but it wasn't until later in life that I sorted my teeth out and capped them all. I remember having a night brace at one time, to straighten my teeth out, but the dogs, to their delight, discovered it and chewed it up when I left it on my bedside table. It was never replaced.

The dogs' teeth were in a bit of a state, too. Actually, after a while, they had no teeth left to attack the post or my brace with. Perhaps it's because they loved the toffees so much—or rather my friends and I did. Part of the fun would be to test the toffees on the dogs and watch the poor creatures screw up their faces as their jaws stuck together. In the end, they just couldn't be bothered to chew anything at all and swallowed most sweets whole, including bubble gum still in wrappers and a good proportion of the important letters and checks for the ailing family business.

The tiny family publishing business was based in our home. Letters were strewn all over the kitchen table, in drawers, and on the couches, with typewriters on tables and telephones dotted around the ground floor.

Peggy and Sheba, we used to joke, were the complaints department, and no kidding: I saw letters being screwed up and thrown to the dogs, who ripped them up, along with unwanted bills and terrible black and white photos of marketing directors with huge collars who wanted their faces published in the magazine. Everything was left in pieces across the floor. It was definitely the worst way to publish magazines and run a business, but there were no laws or rules, and everyone did as they pleased. It's actually astonishing the company survived.

Peggy was called *Peggy* because one leg didn't work very well from when she was a puppy, and she always had one ear up and one down and couldn't hear too well, which explains why she never did anything that was asked of her. You used to say "sit," and she would simply get up, limp away, and focus on doing the entirely opposite of whatever you asked her.

On vacations, she was part of the family with the cringeworthy kids and the embarrassing dogs that would chase sheep all over Welsh farms while you were trying to have a quiet picnic, enjoy the view, and go unnoticed. We lived in dread that a local farmer would leap over a stone wall with his shotgun and take our dogs out.

Sheba was Peggy's mother, and her trick was to chew the lovely Edwardian sash windows in the house when you opened them. She had a thing about windows and car seat belts, which added to the general madness of our house. As soon as you opened a window, she would race into the room and leap toward the base of the sash, hang from it without her back legs even touching the ground, and bite it furiously. Absolutely nuts!

There wasn't really any one moment when we became that crazy candy family in the leafy plane-tree suburbs of North London. We were just always a bit odd from the beginning. There was a reason, I guess, for the neglect of my well-being. But, no, don't worry! This is not an I-was-an-ignored-child book. Far from it; some say I could claim title to the best childhood ever—free sweets all the time and a mother who hardly knew or cared if I went to school.

I didn't think much about being different until later on. When I started senior school at eleven years old, I discovered that my friends had things like clean bedrooms, ironed clothes, and other curiosities. I was used to being able to write my name in the dust under my bed and surviving with one clean pair of socks a week. The socks would stand up stiff without bending by Friday.

However, the layers of dust had been like this for many years. Years before my father contracted cancer, I developed a nasty lung condition called pleurisy, when I was six years old, that nearly killed me before him.

My diet was terrible for as long as I can remember, since my mother had always been drinking. She boasted that she drank Guinness when she was pregnant with me, right from the start. So even at the age of six, there were times when the candy was all there *was* to eat—so it was unsurprising that I fell ill occasionally. But I knew this illness was bad when my relations started turning up at the front door with presents and all sorts of goodies, even store-bought candies. They were a rare thing; we Kennedys *never* had to buy sweets.

I was left in the living room, where I could hear friends and relations sniffling and blowing their noses outside the door. I must have looked a bit rough. They talked as if they might not see me again. Even the hospital staff nurses came out to me rather than having me go to them, so I knew something was up. But at least I finally received some attention, another relatively rare commodity in the house.

There was a lot of whispering behind the living room door during my home hospital experience. I didn't know it, but I was on the way out. The dust had taken its toll on me. I was moved down to the living room for weeks on end. I think my mum realized that the bedroom full of dust was not such a good idea.

I had lost the use of my left lung. I was nearly gone. When you are seriously ill, you don't actually know how close you are to the end, especially when you are young. It's a bit of a novelty. You just think it's cool that the headmistress comes around to say hello and brings a present from the class with a signed card from all your friends saying, "Come back soon, we miss you."

People around me seemed to be doing a lot of crying, which was a bit puzzling. I must have been close to death, but at the time I felt beautifully dizzy—there was no pain, but it was difficult to breathe. A nurse visited every day from the hospital. Each morning, I would lay on my stomach while she massaged my back, pressing hard, and with every push these hideous dollops of brown rubbery phlegm would come firing out of my lungs and into a saucepan on the floor. I'm guessing it was probably not washed up afterward and used to boil the vegetables.

The discharge from my lungs was so hard that these hideous rubbery missiles almost bounced out of the saucepan, much to the dogs' delight. They were never too far away to make further investigations into any new types of textured food.

I remember going "spacey" as I lay down on the couch one afternoon, staring as the ceiling rose. I found everything and everyone a little distant and dreamy. I could sleep for hours with no wish to get up. My body had become part of the stationary elements of the room. I remained on my couch, staring at the black-and-white TV and gazing at the cobwebs forming around the ceiling, for weeks on end.

I knew every inch and every crack of the room from my position, and as the days passed, I felt I was becoming part of the room and no longer a mobile, active part of everyday life.

As you can imagine, my health was probably suspect before I got the lung infection. My bedroom was so cold the ice was often on the inside of the window, and my bed was right next to the windows, but I think that was common in those days. We didn't have central heating; it was all coal and gas. To this day, I can sleep anywhere, no matter how cold it is.

I was also quite overweight at six years old. It's just as well, really, because I lost a lot of weight while sick. I remember lying down day after day, watching *Hector's House* and *The Magic Roundabout* kids' programs and refusing to eat anything for weeks; nothing, not even a single American jelly bean or a licorice-flavored Black Jack chew. There comes a point when you decide if you want life. They can try to rescue you with all the medications they like, but you have to be a part of the rescue.

It's a beautiful feeling, drifting off to the other side—so much better than Earth. I am not frightened of death. I have been close to its embrace on at least two other occasions, and here, with a lung infection and antibiotics not working, I could see why there was a sea of cards and cuddly toys on the mantelpiece over the nasty gas fire that was put there in place of a beautiful Victorian-tiled open fireplace.

There is something about inhabiting a body that has no wish to move that enables its inhabitant to tune into it. The silence speaks— you can hear your blood pumping through your veins. A bit of peace is something that I only dream of nowadays with my five children.

But I never once believed I would die. Being unaware of being ill saved me, really; ignorance of what can polish you off can be a great form of medicine. I had a friend at college who seemed healthy and very happy. She went to see a doctor for a routine test, was told she had cancer, got really depressed, and soon after that passed away. I am sure the chemo and the anxiety killed her. I often think she might have lived with the cancer if she had not known she had it. Just like I lay there on death's door but quite happy, without the thought of ever dying.

The decision to get up and live again seemed to be within me. I was drifting peacefully, waking up and not knowing where I was lying, and then the great day for my mum's diary took place. One morning, my mother wobbled into the room, trying hard to look positive and to hide her despair while carrying the daily hopefully-this-time breakfast that she had lovingly prepared on a tray.

Each breakfast had new things to eat, laid out differently. Sometimes there were handwritten "get better" notes, or toys, or anything to help wake me up and take an interest. She was running out of ideas and I was running out of time, something of which she was acutely aware.

She must have blamed herself for ignoring the dust building up and the cold temperature of my bedroom. She would never have forgiven herself if I had left her.

But that morning, I asked for one of my favorites at the time. It was a toss-up between a Curly Wurly and a tube of Smarties.

"Mum, can I have some Smarties?"

The words took a moment or two for her to register, as my simple statement seemed to hit her like an alien magnetic force field.

She nearly dropped the whole tray of breakfast as she stood in front of me with her mouth open and a look of uncontrollable panic at the thought I might change my mind. She placed the tray on the coffee table while the dogs moved in and hugged my emaciated body so tightly my ribs nearly met from both sides. There was such a commotion. It was like she didn't have a second to spare in case I really did change my mind, fall asleep, or succumb to some other dreadful inconvenience like dying.

She grabbed the tray and ran into the kitchen, bacon and all sorts of goodies flying off in her wake, to the complete delight of the frenzied pets, who followed the trail of descending goodies. She searched frantically for some Smarties in the kitchen drawers. I could hear her pull them so hard, I was sure they would come clean out of the cabinet.

Not finding any, my mother grabbed the keys to her brilliantly underpowered Renault 4, skipped out the door, revved the tiny 950-cc engine so much I thought the car would explode, and raced up to the corner shop on Highgate Hill. She returned with the sacred candies, tore the lid off the tube with pieces firing in all directions, handed it to me with her shaking hand, froze, and then waited in great anticipation for me to start eating them without taking her eyes off me.

Another unavoidable and almost crippling hug came my way, and then she was quickly on the phone to tell "Mother." She always called her mum "Mother."

"He's eating, yes, Angus, he's eating now," she screamed into the phone. It was a truly great day to have one less name on Muswell Hill's homemade death row list.

She really did love me; she did care a great deal about her kids. To this day I never blame anyone with a drinking problem. People with alcohol dependency do not love you any less, even though it seems that way. The love is always there, deep down behind all the booze and confusion.

It takes some wisdom to see through it all. Better surely to have a drug addict who loves you than a healthy parent who doesn't. Ironically, I learned more from my mother than I would have if she had been in good health, and I can't blame her for the way she was. You have to be very strong to deal with the forces that drive you to drink. Moreover, you can't blame yourself for not being able to rescue anyone from it. They alone can make that final decision, just like I did, in a way, when I decided that the mini-Wonka would live on!

After my first close shave with my maker, I tried not to inhabit my body for illness anymore. It doesn't really matter what the illness means—what matters is the meaning we give to the illness. If you survive, you learn; if you die, they learn. At last I was on the slow road to recovery. The chocolate treats that I had eaten to fatten me up before may well have saved my life. It's difficult to finish off a candy kid.

My mum changed a little after realizing that my immersion in dust was not of great use to me or the rest of my family. I considered my brother, James, two years older than me, the lucky one, as shortly thereafter he went to boarding school. My half sister, Helen, from my mother's first marriage, was eleven years older than me, and it wasn't much longer before she was off to university and I was left in the house.

However, after a short respite, the dust and mess reaccumulated, causing another looming problem. This time it was in my bedroom, where another close shave was on its way, ready to take me away in the middle of the night. It wasn't long after the pleurisy; I was still six years old.

If you have ever woken up to flames in your bedroom, you will never forget that noise or the terrifying sight reaching to the top of your walls.

After my lung condition was diagnosed, I had been given a breathing apparatus that basically consisted of a "placed candle" under some waxy substance to keep some liquid hot and airborne, I guess to help me breathe at night. I hated it. It was the size of a small saucer and could be placed anywhere near the patient. My parents were so frightened of me contracting a lung infection again that they were adamant about this new routine. By trying to save me, they were unwittingly planning another potential casualty.

So, every night a live flame was placed on my bedroom mantel-piece, next to a few cuddly toys and old Airfix model boxes, to burn until the following morning. Above it were posters stuck on with dried Blu Tack that always came down, and around it were all sorts of other very-willing-to-ignite articles and tubes of glue. I guess it was bound to happen at some point. I'm not an expert on house fires, but it seems like in the 1970s just about anything in your bedroom could catch alight rapidly.

If you have suffered a house fire at night in your youth, you may never sleep soundly, no matter how old you become. You wake to any noise. Since the night my room caught fire, I have always been a very light sleeper.

I am not sure how I woke up. There was so much smoke, I should have been unconscious. I found myself sitting up in bed watching the magnificent display of huge orange flames burning up the curtains at the side of each window. The flames were so hot and I only had the covers to keep the heat away. Everywhere I looked it seemed there were flames licking everything, and I was having trouble staying focused as my blanket and sheets started to catch fire at the edges.

In such a situation, you might want to scream as loudly as possible, but my voice was hoarse and weak from the smoke, and I felt confused and dizzy. It was a miracle I was sitting up in bed at all.

It wasn't long before I couldn't really see anyway; I was short of breath and unable to move. I wanted to scream but I couldn't. There was so little oxygen that nothing seemed to work in my body. *Doesn't anyone know I am going to die (again)?* I thought. *I want my dad, my mum, anyone.*

In a house fire, you're likely to pass out and suffocate long before you fry, but I was awake as the flames worked their way up the wall, sizzling the woolen blankets in search of their grandest prize of all—a human life.

The noise was terrifying. Cracking, spitting, small things in the room popping, wooden curtain poles falling off the walls: you never forget the deathly noises of being so close to a fire.

Where's my mum? Is there no one there? Where's my dad? Are my parents dead too? Help me, please, God, help me.

I could think but not act. I was going to pass out, be the fuel and not the victim.

My mum always slept heavily, as she was likely unconscious from the bottles of anything she had left that day. My dad was a big man with a heart of gold. Though none of us knew it, he was soon to be struggling with cancer. Was I going to be the one welcoming him to heaven first?

There was a huge crash. A wall coming down, a ceiling, I don't know. A blast of some sort? I heard screaming, my name being called out. My bedroom door flew off its hinges, and this time it was Dad's turn to save Angus. My angel and my hero stood strong at the doorway, and what a magnificent display it was to see him there with the door lying on the floor at his feet.

He flew across my room to rescue me from that burning hell. I was in my dad's arms, wrapped up in a cold blanket and whisked down the stairs to the sounds of sirens and the imminent arrival of the emergency services.

After being close to death a few times, I am not scared of it. I should be dead, so I just think I am lucky. Anyway, it's not the length of the life that matters, it's how much we can teach before we die.

It turned out it was only a fire in the bedroom and hadn't spread at all, so what seemed like the whole house burning down to me, was just the curtains and a few posters. My father extinguished it easily, and it wasn't long before things were back to normal. Though my school friends were never sure what to expect when I next came into class. This time, they really thought I was a spectacle returning to school after being starved, baked, and asphyxiated. There was never a normal entry to school for me at any time, something I just got used to. I guess nothing has changed, even today.

The lung infection and the house fire left a half-baked, nutritionally starved, candy-laden kid on the block; my general health was affected even a few years later. And as the time passed, I had to watch out for another hazard—the less conventional ways of cooking my mother employed.

Eating was another near-death experience. It was almost a race to see who would go first: my dad, mother, or me. We were all truly excellent candidates for what now seemed to be regular appointments with potential death.

CHAPTER 2

Candy to the Rescue

And so, we all made it, together, for another four years after the fire. My mother was suitably satisfied that we, including the dogs, were still enjoying the added bonus of being alive. I am sure that by this time she knew of my father's illness, which must have started when I was nine, and which only made her drinking worse.

Dinner at home was a fairly suicidal affair if you weren't careful. It was an achievement to make it from six years old to nine in my house. In between rescuing the mail and having a candy fix, my new survival test involved fighting an enemy that was smaller than a raging inferno—the bacteria in my food, in what little eventually found its way to my plate. My mother didn't have much time to cook, as she was busy trying to work, too.

The problem with publishing is that there is never enough advertising to go around. It's still the same today; selling magazine advertisements is a high-pressure job. I have sold millions of pounds' worth, and it's still just as hard convincing someone today to buy something they don't really want as it was then. She was always going back to the phone or her homemade minibar and giving either a go, and they were both brilliant distractions from cooking.

Meanwhile, I was always going hungry and my poor father was getting weaker by the month with his cancer. Often, cooking occurred only when my mother remembered to, and it was quite an education. Every now and then we enjoyed a truly great meal, as she really could cook once upon a time, but sadly the drink molded her into the very last person you would want to accept a dinner invite from.

I used to have to do a kind of excavation job on my dinner plate to see what was waiting for me among chunks of raw garlic, orange or lemon peel, and hundreds of cloves or countless peppercorns (she always spilled the packet). Or worse still, I would be presented with reheated food that was several days or even weeks old, in which case it was not unusual to find myself sharing a plate with the occasional maggot or other insectoid dinner guests.

My mother's disastrous cooking techniques advanced considerably, especially in the evenings when she really could not even recognize the contents of the cooking pots she was tending to. She continued to add ingredients at random times, as she couldn't remember how long had passed since she had started cooking, or if the gas burner was on at all.

She liked curry, so you can imagine how hot some of those dishes became when she cooked with triple doses of chili powder. To this day, my brother and I like a hot curry. I also continue to check my food for bugs (cooked or alive) that might have taken a liking to my dinner or anything else: from stones or hundreds of peppercorns to household items like lids of ingredients jars or random items of cutlery that might have accidentally fallen into the cooking pot.

Mum sometimes even forgot she was cooking at all, and would wobble straight past the burning pots to the end of the kitchen, where a convenient gin bottle was handy to help her through the day. She never forgot about that.

It was a fine occasion to have the real meal deal that was both tasty and edible. Even if it was a good dish—because she could be a fabulous cook—sadly she would often fall asleep (well, pass out) while it cooked. I would rush downstairs through the smoke to find the spaghetti burned dry and retire to my bedroom to nibble on a Tunnock's Teacake. I saved those for special no-dinner-from-Mum-this-time occasions.

Sometimes I thought I had quite exceeded myself with an excellent idea to feed Peggy and Sheba with the dinners that were not, in my opinion, fit for us humans. But they would have none of it. The blasted dogs knew better. They'd run away from under the kitchen table when presented with a human's plate, just in case I tried to feed them.

I had the most intolerable stomach pains most days after school. They became so severe that while waiting at the bus stop on the way home from school, I would buy a warm, freshly baked loaf of bread from the baker, who was strategically positioned right next to the bus stop. I would then eat the whole thing outside the bakery while waiting for the Route 134 London double-decker, only to realize when the bus finally arrived that I had spent my bus fare.

It was never really established what caused the pains, as I don't recall seeing a doctor about it. I expect now, after having kids of my own, that it was threadworms. It was also a several-mile walk from London's Camden Town to Muswell Hill, so I probably used up all my calories walking home.

Needless to say, I would turn to my private candy store and fuel up on sugary carbohydrates. The large supply of free confectionery really was my savior, essential to keeping me alive during my school years. I lived off the stuff, which I kept in cardboard boxes locked in the cupboard in my room. On many occasions, it pretty much saved my life.

I know what it's like to be hungry, and nowadays I never leave anything on my plate and always save everything after the family meal.

The best times were definitely the nights my mother returned home with so many sweets in the car that the rear bumper scraped along the road. Things were looking especially good when she managed to trade the tiny Renault 4 for a Ford Cortina XL with velour seats, a real cassette player, a cigarette lighter, and an armrest in the back, which seemed an absolute luxury. But most importantly, it had a bigger trunk, which meant one thing—a larger hoard of candies.

Yes, an entire car jam-packed with sweets straight from the largest confectionery show in Europe. Possibly every kid's dream? I knew that I would be able to stock up for weeks with such a hoard, and that it would keep me going right through the winter. My mother, as a journalist, would be handed plenty of free products at the trade show in Cologne, Germany, which I now visit every year myself.

In fact, I have been attending this show since the age of twelve. It's an enormous trade fair, where you can walk through fifteen halls the size of cricket pitches and pass a thousand trade stands displaying the world's tastiest confectionery and bakery products. At the trade exhibition, you can eat and take home as much as you can carry. I go every year, and like my mother did before me, I come home with a car filled to the brim with the best French, Swiss, Belgian, Italian, and German chocolate on the market, although today I have five willing kids to help unload when I return. I also have a rather bashed up twelve-year-old Toyota Land Cruiser Invincible that can hold a welcome two thousand pounds, so I am very well-equipped for our candy cargo. I take magazines to the show and return with a carful of every possible treat you can imagine.

The tradition carries on, from generation to generation. My kids wait for me to return from Germany with a load of goodies, and I know exactly how they feel. They say, "Dad, where're the sweets?" not, "Hi, Dad, did you have a good time? How was the show?" But I know how exciting it is at that age. My children make a homemade supermarket with the products I bring back from the show and we all pretend to buy and sell them, which makes a great game, especially when one of them (my five-year-old) is bottom in Math. When he has to work out how much money will buy a packet of his favorite Haribo marshmallows, he soon realizes math can be exquisitely useful.

I return with so much product that I could build a mini-mountain out of all the goodies. Last year, my son took some of it to his school the day after my return for his chemistry teacher's birthday, while my younger son took a packet of expensive Italian wafers to share with his ten-year-old friends. So, in a way, I am creating popular Wonkas at their schools. My daughters, on the other hand, just got on with the important job of actually eating the stuff, going so far as to consume white chocolate with macadamia nuts for breakfast.

We trade with chocolate, too. For example, this weekend a friend who practices Reiki healing came over to work on my wife and me. After the session was over, I handed her a massive bag of Italian chocolates that I was given the week before, fresh from the factory in the Dolomites mountains, in exchange for her work in clearing my chakras. Seemed like a good deal to me. She was delighted, though her five-year-old son managed to dig into the bag before she did.

I give people chocolate all the time. They are often too polite to ask for it, and sometimes it does seem a little silly giving just a small bag of candies to say thanks for something. But they are really happy and nearly always overreact, as if I have given them a bottle of vintage French champagne. But maybe they genuinely are thrilled, not least because I am thinking of them and thanking people with sweets and not words, which I must admit makes a difference. If all else fails, try chocolate!

As a child, I knew the arrival of the car in the middle of the night was my supply ship coming in. It would provide the lion's share of my annual hoard, survival items and things to trade with at school. I would circle the car, like a squirrel rushing through a walnut tree, and grab packets of chips, endless boxes of jellies and chews, and all manner of goodies without even looking at the labels, rush upstairs to my room, throw a decent batch of them into my bedroom cupboard, slam the door, and lock it tight.

In the meantime, my mother would get out of the car in need of an immediate drink, so yours truly attended to the job at hand. My task was to empty the rest of the Ford Cortina and carry the bags of sweets up a flight of stairs and into the living room. Like every room of our house, the living room was never cleaned, so I pushed everything to the side to make way for the incoming cargo. I emptied bag after bag and made a huge pile of goodies on the floor, everything and anything: Black Jacks, Spangles, penny chews, French nougat, Opal Fruits, pear drops, halva, Love Hearts, Jelly Belly beans, Walker's toffee (which came with a metal hammer to break it with), and loads of other goodies. There were even the most exquisite embossed tins of Walkers and Campbells shortbreads, which really came in handy for storing Lego and Meccano pieces. I would also receive products that were yet to be launched around the world and be the first kid in not just the UK, but sometimes the whole planet to try them.

The house would once again be most conveniently fueled up with candy, biscuits, chocolates, chews, and some really weird products with lettering in Arabic or another language that I couldn't work out. But I didn't care one hoot; this was my booty. You name it, Mum had it in the car. Manufacturers gave her just about as much as she could carry. She never ate any of it. Both my brother and my sister were living and studying away from home by now, so almost every last piece was for the budding Wonka to sample.

I was so proud of my mum, and her making it home without crashing was a favorable bonus all round. She often drove alone in the middle of the night across Europe, and I knew that I was the one she was coming home to. I knew she would not have carried on if it wasn't for my waiting for her. My brother, sister, and I were her reason for staying alive, which was hard work for her when she knew she was dying a painfully slow and inevitable death.

But when she came home late at night, it was just so amazing to see her do something for us like that. I knew she collected all these sweets from the trade show for her son Angus and my brother in boarding school and sister at university. That's why she really got them.

She would stand there in the living room, watching me and smiling as I ripped open all the bulging carrier bags of sweets in astonishment, and I would tell her, "Mum, you are amazing." She didn't hear me say that often, and I saw the tears in the corners of her eyes. If only I could have said it more: *Mum, you are amazing.* I wish I had. It was those rare moments I said she was special that were very special for both of us. After she died, this became what I remember and hold close.

We are never really that proud of our parents, but there are pockets in time when we see how hard it really is for them to get it right and keep going on and on day after day, fighting the impossible systems put before them. I was proud that she managed to stay alive. It was that simple; she fought every day to stay alive and be with us.

We had many foreign products from Egypt, Syria, Greece, the United States, India, Grenada, and all sorts of other wacky places I'd never heard of or had seen only in pictures in scuffed geography textbooks. It was the best way to learn geography. But all those sweets, when I look back, were very different from today's.

A lot of the candy companies that existed then have been acquired or are now out of business. The world of confectionery has changed a good deal, but of course it has, as has the rest of the world. This was a few years before we bought our first Apple Macintosh Plus computer with which to publish. Fry's and Rowntree's were independent companies that were, like Cadbury, founded on Victorian Quakerism. There were a number of large food companies that were founded by people with such strong faith. That was in the days before death duties and new employment laws existed, and the owners of businesses amassed huge private wealth and built their fabulous English mansions.

Fry's was bought by Cadbury and then Cadbury by Mondelēz (Kraft Heinz), but I still remember when Fry's was independent. Believe it or not, they were the first company to invent the molded chocolate bar in 1847. Yes, Fry's invented our chocolate bar, and few people know it. It also invented Fry's Turkish Delight, a chocolate-enrobed, rose hip–flavored gelatin countline bar, still made by Cadbury—and it was another product I had available on regular call in my school blazer's inside pocket.

Meanwhile, Rowntree's, which is from York in the United Kingdom, invented some of the world's best-known brands in the 1930s—including none other than Kit Kat (1935). Hershey acquired the rights to produce Kit Kat in 1978, and today it is one of the world's biggest selling confectionery brands. Reports say they now sell around 250,000 every day! Yes, all from a small factory in York.

Rowntree's also invented Aero, Smarties, and Quality Street in the 1930s. I always found that a small yellow box of their colorful Fruit Pastilles would make a bad movie a good one; they were first produced by Rowntree's well over one hundred years ago, in 1881.

When gobble-up time began, they merged with another British company that is all but forgotten, Mackintosh. Then Rowntree's bought a whole load of other companies, including Tom's Foods, Sunmark confectionery, and more, and then (deep breath), along comes Nestlé in 1988, who gobbled them all up in one delicious gulp. Bang, gone, amen, lest we forget.

I always had some Rowntree's Fruit Pastilles in my blazer. You could go into a corner shop and see their name on large glass jars on the shelves among other products such as Terry's All Gold chocolates, Bassett's Liquorice Allsorts, Mackintosh's Egg and Milk Toffees, Anglo Bubbly bubble gums, Paynes Poppets, Maynards Wine Gums, and Barker & Dobson Television Selection. Really—they had a tin of sweets with a picture of a family all watching TV together as the big occasion. The tins alone are worth around $265 on eBay now, so if you find one, hang onto it. Anyway, these are names I have engrained in my mind to this day, and soon many will perhaps be remembered only with a trip back in time to my dusty attic.

It wasn't long ago that what I would estimate was most of our sugar confectionery was presented in large glass jars on shelves behind store counters. You could pop down to your local sweetshop (which existed then), point to your favorite jar on the shelf, and be served your quarter pound of Humbugs. You'd see them weighed on a scale and placed in a paper bag. I would keep mine in my pocket at school all day. Almost everything came in a jar, from lollipops to sugar mice. No one thought of having them available in a different format.

That was until the late 1970s, when a company called Haribo came along and, thinking ahead, realized that they could argue it was not entirely hygienic for fingers and scoops to go in and out of the sweets jars all day long. They packaged their jellies in small, individual, hermitically sealed cellophane bags. Newly available packing technologies could weigh and deposit exact amounts of jellies into tiny bags by the thousands. They're actually called *multihead weighers*, and these amazing machines took the industry by storm. They could cope with high volumes of small packs at exactly the right weight and then drop the jellies into a superfast, vertical-form seal packaging (bagging) machine that fired the packs out at the speed of a machine gun. Today's machines can do around three hundred a minute.

No one paid Haribo much attention at first. Then in the late 1970s, terms such as *food contamination* and *product safety* became more critical and began entering the early workplace manuals. The new machines unfortunately also meant less labor, as shop assistants didn't have to measure or weigh products from jars. It was a win-win. The factories could have fewer people working for them, the retailers could do other things with their time, and there was no food contamination (which I believe there wasn't in the first place) caused by scoops and spoons.

By the time many other producers realized what was going on, the new packaging used by Haribo and other early adopters had changed the landscape of our corner confectionery shop forever and gradually the jars disappeared. By the end of the 1970s, jars had given way almost entirely to prepacked products in bags, and companies that were not fast enough to realize this trend did not survive. The industry went through a quiet but huge revolution in packaging.

However, my room at home needed no sealed packs, as most of the stash was taken straight to school for trading. The legendary "sweet mountain," as we called it, would be piled high in our living room, higher than our black-and-white television, which never worked very well anyway. (That was in the days when, to get our TV going, I would have to bang it hard on the top and then stand on the end of the couch while dangling the utterly useless antenna off the side of the curtain rails at such an angle that we could actually watch it.)

My new hoard of confectionery contained all the power in the world for a nine-year-old boy. I was the Candy King. Chocolate still has a magical power, even for adults. I believe in its magic; I am still alive and that's proof.

I was the boy who could bring any type of confectionery to school, at will and to order. This gave me a lot of confidence and a great deal of popularity. Even back then I was often called the Wonka boy. Who isn't popular when they always give away free sweets? I was a living fairy tale: a cross between Robin Hood and the Pied Piper, and living in the witch's house from *Hansel and Gretel*.

Returning to school after any period of time, after a fire, illness, or simply because my mother did not take me in for a while, would always spark curiosity. My mother would pull the car up outside the rusty iron Victorian school gates, and I knew that my arrival would always be different from the other kids'. I walked into the schoolyard, which had surprisingly little to play with considering it was said to house our playground—just some old car tires to roll around the yard and high brick fences. It was a claustrophobic place, but I could always brighten it up with the copious amount of sweets stuffed into my leather satchel and my pocketfuls of Gobstoppers and penny chews. In an instant, children came running across the schoolyard, caps flying off their heads, to get in with the kid with candy. Hypnotized by the treats, they pulled on my blazer, tried to open my satchel, and demanded free sweets.

Well not *so* free. Some pieces were given away, but others, like the new products not yet on the market, were definitely for trading. And here I learned a very important life lesson, namely how to trade and negotiate.

I must have appeared a rare human sample, a frail, pale, and gangly version of what I once was, but nevertheless I was capable of conjuring curiosity from all corners of the school. And from the overused school-yard to the sickly powdered egg–smelling dining halls, kids appeared like ants to view the spectacle and land some sweets from the school's very own Wonka.

"Roll up," I would holler. "Angus Kennedy, an original sight, a somewhat different Angus is here, everyone," I accentuated with a raspy voice from a lung condition years ago to add to the special effects.

I felt great at these times. I was a mess, of course, but I didn't see it. My candy lifted my spirits and everyone else's for that matter. I made people happy, I still do today, and that's all that will ever matter to me. I was determined to be with my classmates and get on with the tasks of swapping, eating, and demonstrating the newest sweets in the land.

School was all about laughing, playing Ace Trumps card games (sports cars edition), and having fun. It was a forgone conclusion that I would fail most, if not all, of my exams. But success was always weaved into the accomplishment of happiness.

Oddly, I never really felt *that* ill with pleurisy or from my other random dalliances with death. I never thought I was going to die in the fire, or let some ghastly intestinal worms take me either. These were all just annoying inconveniences. Kids are the best teachers; they are masters of enjoying the present, while adults are masters of not getting over the past, or worrying about illness.

Throughout everything, above all, I looked forward to going back to swooning over the amazing girls in class, one of whom I hopelessly fell in love with. I was back at "work" feeding kids with treats while trying to catch the attention of my heart's desire, the latest beautiful girl with whom I was completely mesmerized. But as the weeks went by, I was unaware of the inevitable.

Soon, even desperate crushes would be obliterated from my thoughts. I don't know anyone else who has ever had a Christmas quite like the one I was about to experience. All the presents were under the tree, but I didn't want to open them. A horrible feeling of foreboding had come over me. For the first time in my life, I was truly scared. I just knew something horrible was about to happen. I wanted time to freeze and for the tree to be there and the presents remain unopened so life could be put on hold forever.

CHAPTER 3

My Father's Death

In short time, all I was to have left of my dad would be the few badly developed black-and-white photos leaning against my bedside lamp. If only I could have taken more photos. I would gaze at a picture of the two of us on holiday on a beach together for hours before sleep, imagining him until he was really with me. But there was no way the pictures could tuck me in, pull my duvet up, and kiss me good night.

I had to remember that it's not the length of a life that counts: a short life as a good man is always better than a long life as a bad one. We never learn from a perfect life.

The death of your father, particularly when you are nine years old, fries your circuit boards and reprograms you in an instant. If I had been a computer on that Christmas Eve, I might have been thrown out the window from the fourth floor onto reinforced concrete (for good measure).

You are left with the bits of your old life scattered in places you will never find them. You know whatever you do put back together can't ever be the same. Perhaps my dad and I had struck a deal with our maker before we came to Earth: "Okay, Angus," God would have said. "It's going to be a tough one, but I'll give you a life's supply of chocolate, mate." Life was okay—the odd mishap and a wonky mum, tons of chocolate and candies—but to be honest on that day I would have not minded dying too.

But life *is* worth dying for.

———————

Other kids at school had been dished out far worse than I had experienced—something I always tried to convince myself of, even though I found it hard. There was one particular girl at school for example, Sarah, who had the most terrible purple rash on one whole side of her face. From the very first day she turned up at school, she was bullied constantly, day after day. She used to hide away at the edge of the playground with her head down. One day, after a year at school, Sarah never came back in through the gates. We found out a few days later that she had committed suicide. She could have only been about ten years old. It hurts now to think about it, how cruel we are. If only I could have given her some sweets, just once . . . but I didn't. I regret it.

I still hate myself for having been so inhumane as to ignore her, just in the same way as the other kids took no notice. I will regret that always. Maybe all it would have taken was just one single sweet from my huge hoard. I try not to make these mistakes today. It's never too late to change, to make someone smile.

Winter came, and it was two days before Christmas Eve, December 23, 1973. It seemed odd that my mother had arranged for me to have a sleepover with my best friend so close to Christmas. I didn't know my father was *that ill*, but I had noticed he had been sitting in his big, paisley armchair for unusually long periods of time, watching TV (after I bashed it) and not being very active. I always assumed it was a minor illness and he would get better. I learned later he was on morphine.

A bonus sleepover was on offer, an unexpected treat to stay over with my best friend, who lived across the road, a couple of days before the big day when we opened the presents. Yes, a double-good Christmas. What an occasion! I ran up the stairs to see my dad sitting in the living room and said a quick goodbye.

I didn't even kiss him, just shouted my final farewell from across the room in the doorway. I didn't really notice his hand sticking out at the side of the chair, beckoning me closer. He knew it was the last time he would ever see his son, but I was in a hurry to have fun.

If only I had kissed him, seen him again, hugged him, understood him, or touched his hand, anything, but it wasn't to be. I might have seen the tears on his face that my mother told me about years after his death. I still think how painful that must have been for him to see me run out the door, without him having the chance to say goodbye. What atomic strength a parent must possess to see their nine-year-old child leave the room, knowing it's the last time they will see him and the last time their son will be happy for months or years. To me, the hardest thing possible for any man to endure is knowing you are going to die and watching your kids play and laugh when you know it's inevitable that one day yours will be among the saddest kids on the planet and you won't be there to comfort them.

He looked pale and withdrawn. Just a winter virus, I thought.

"I love you, Angus," he said as I headed for the door. He took a moment to compose himself. "You'll look after your mum, won't you, Angus?"

It seemed odd he would say something like that. He had never said it before.

"See you tomorrow, Dad," I replied.

It went quiet. I spotted his arm from the back of the armchair reaching out for me, but I was going for a sleepover and it was fun, fun, fun. Off I ran, down the stairs with my carefully selected sleepover candies. If only I had known, I would have stayed.

I am sure my mother found it too painful to watch our last meeting. She was waiting in the hall at the bottom of the stairs looking solemn and not saying a word. Clearly she thought I wasn't strong enough to stay home and see him die. I raced downstairs, but this time no dogs chased after me, even though they *always* did. Instead, they lay quietly by my father's side, refusing to move. If only I had done the same.

Wow, what a strange day it is, I thought as I grabbed my sleeping bag in the hallway and said goodbye to my mum. She reached out her hand to try and grab me. But I just held her hand quickly, gave her a kiss, and was on my way across the road.

My friend's mother was there on the pavement outside our house to meet me, and she was extra friendly. That was a bit odd, too, as she never came to our door to pick me up or chat.

Even more special, I thought, *she's being really nice; gonna be a great Christmas then*. It was time to go and have fun.

My friend and I stayed awake into the early hours of the morning talking about what we were going to get for Christmas, especially the *big* present from our dads. I would always take a stash of sweets over on sleepovers and it was a special occasion to have a midnight feast and lay all the chocolates and treats over the floor while the parents were sleeping. My kids do this today.

The next morning, I sat at the breakfast table munching through my Sugar Puffs while reading the packet about the Honey Monster out loud to my friend and laughing. I could hear my friend's mother on the phone in the hall just beside the door to the lounge we were eating in. Her voice was quiet and subdued. She hung up, came into the room, and walked over to the cooker.

That must have been some argument she had, I thought as she

came over to put the scrambled eggs on the table. Then she walked over and put her hand on my shoulder. I thought it was even more strange for her to do that. My friend and I just giggled.

"Mum, you okay?" asked my friend, looking puzzled.

She said nothing and went back to the kitchen to work out her next move.

"Think I had better go," I said to my friend.

Of course, his mother knew that the next time she saw me she would see a broken kid who wouldn't smile for months. She was almost speechless. My dad was my rock.

I got home, and my mother was waiting in the hall. I knew instantly that something terrible had happened.

"Angus, it's dad; he's gone." There was a long pause as she tried to compose herself. "He's gone somewhere beautiful, Angus, a place where he will be really happy." Now she was struggling to talk. "Angus, it's your father; he's gone," she repeated.

She couldn't bring herself to say the word "dead," but she carried on talking. I got the odd words like "cancer," "sorry," and "died," but now my head was spinning like a hornet's nest. I wanted to hide, escape, or die. Surely, she was drunk again. He'll come back *of course* from this "somewhere beautiful."

And so came the end of the first chapter of my life. I wanted a nice new one, a life without chocolate and candy, even. Yes, I would never eat sweets ever again, I promised, I would say to my gods, if only it meant being able to have him back.

Christmas Day came, and there I sat in disbelief in the lounge, staring at the empty chair where my father used to sit. Now crying uncontrollably, I reached out for my present to him, not knowing whom to give it to as I held it in my shaking hands. I put it down and took a big present from under the tree to console myself and read the label.

"Happy Christmas, my beautiful son, I love you so much. Dad"

I stared at the sunken hollow in the chair where he had sat for so long, and then I opened his present to me. It was a tennis racket, the last present I ever received from my father, from a man I hardly had time to get to know. I sat on the carpet holding the racket, with my mother crying in the background watching over me. I dreamed of the days when I was the ball boy running around the tennis court in our local park, handing balls to my father when he was so fit and strong and smiling back at me. I desperately held onto all I had left, images and memories of his smiling face.

I threw my fist of earth onto the oak lid of my father's coffin and watched the last evidence of my dad go down forever. I wanted to be with him at the bottom of the grave.

For the next few weeks and even after the funeral, I spent a lot of time by the drafty front door waiting and hoping for my dad to come home. Perhaps there had been some kind of mistake? After all, my mother was drunk *all* the time, especially now! And, well, she had probably lost it completely and forgotten he had just gone away for a few days and it was the wrong man in the grave. I thought of anything so I could avoid the truth, and refused to believe he was really gone. Day after day I just wished he would come back.

My crying continued and almost every night I sat in the hallway in the same spot on some boxes of back issues of the family magazine while the dogs looked on, twisting their heads left to right, watching every person that passed our front lounge window. We somehow willed ourselves to believe he would come home again.

Eventually the tears dried up. He wasn't coming home, and I had nothing left. My heart was on the floor, exposed to anyone who wanted to walk over it and kick it aside.

I sunk deeper into my darkness and my mother further into the jaws of her drunken stupors. We scraped along, misfiring at every junction, stalling in and out of our pain. The same questions came up again and again: Why and what could I have done? It was at this point that I felt I had to be a new Angus. The old one would not survive all this. I *had* to make a choice, either go up or down. I think we all have a time to choose the darkness or the light. That's what life is for. Some of us get a lesson a little earlier than others.

This was my biggest potential turning point, but I felt I had nowhere to go and no one to turn to. I was on the verge of giving up, but then two very curious things happened—very strange things indeed.

CHAPTER 4

Strange Visitors to Number 22

A month after the funeral, I woke up in the middle of the night. It was very quiet, and I was fully alert. I couldn't be sure, but I thought I made out the shape of a figure coming through the bedroom door and moving toward me. I was petrified, of course, and yanked the duvet up to my face, ready to dive under the covers until it was much lighter. But an unexpected feeling of calm came over me.

I opened my eyes wider to be sure, and there he was. A tall figure in the dark was coming toward my bed. I couldn't make out a face clearly, but I sensed a paternal presence. He glided across to the side of my bed without any noise or movement of the air. I decided to hide again. This was just plain scary.

There was no conversation, no quick movements or gestures, just a majestic being coming to look over me. My heart was racing. Was it a little silly to call out "Dad?" Could it really be him? The questions were boiling over one after the other.

I still wonder if it could have been an intruder, my mother, or someone else. But I know deep down who it was. I knew right away it was the spirit of my father.

I sat up in bed (still holding the covers to my face) in amazement but feeling this figure radiate its magnificent presence. Everything would be okay, I felt. It's all meant to be, and the being was really very proud of me.

He wasn't there for long, just a minute or so before he vanished. I kept my father's visit my secret for many years afterward. I wouldn't expect anyone to believe me, but whether it was a dream or real, it answered a question for me, and I now know that we live on after death.

When things like this happen to you at such a young age, you start life with an open mind. I now see it as a true blessing. Experiencing my father's passing sculptured me into what I had to be and what I have chosen to be. Death for me is so natural, so normal.

After this death and visitation, and sensing the inescapable looming death of my mother, it was all systems go to find out about life after death, the meaning of life, and what it is for. I possessed a new strength. I had a new sort of personal "dad power."

I realized that if I was careful and responsible with what I asked for, I could ask for anything and it would happen. It works to this day. It has to be something that will be of benefit to humanity; I never ask for money, though I am so tempted (I mean, is it me or have the blasted gas bills tripled?). I have developed this skill considerably. You can call it cosmic ordering, religion, prayer, mind control, law of attraction, or whatever you like—you could get an old pair of underpants to make something happen if you really believe in it.

My father's death was, at least, a learning. Faith is knowing there are always good reasons for bad things, and the only way to learn how to get up again is to keep your mind open. When someone dies on Earth, we may mourn, but they celebrate the return in heaven.

And so I embarked on my mission. I had *big* questions: Why do we die? Why was I born? Why are people so horrible to one another?

Why did my dad die and not the dad of one of my friends? What was so different about me, why me? Where did I go wrong? What does "God" mean? My questions were too much for a desperately inadequate government-set school indoctrination curriculum to answer. Needless to say, when I returned to school, I never wanted to learn anything from my lovely teachers. I only wanted to know why I was singled out so frequently for an alternative life of learning.

Seeing the apparition lifted my spirit, but I struggled as I watched my mother deteriorate. Things went downhill hugely. And then, as if it was all planned, another peculiar thing happened.

———————

Prospects were definitely looking a bit grim. I was now a fatherless and a virtually motherless kid—but hey, *she* was still alive, and that was something. I hung onto my mum, what was left of her anyway. Whether we liked it or not, we were set to survive for the next few years with our self-regulated interruptions of carbs and booze.

I knew I was on rails and approaching a freefall toward a new darkness, a sinister type that I had never experienced. The weeks passed as I continued to wait by the front door for my father.

We had a beautiful original Edwardian stained-glass window set into the top of our oak front door, and normally you could see the fragmented silhouette of the person behind it when they knocked on the door. This time I couldn't see anyone at all after the knocker sounded. How could the bell ring with no one there? It must have been around 7:00 in the evening. It was early in the new year, and I could hear the pathetic whistles and light pops from cheap fireworks sold by the corner shop, the sorts of things the neighbors seemed to think (rather worryingly) were truly amazing.

The hallway was an even bigger mess now: my bicycle was upside down, sitting on its handlebars with a tire puncture that I couldn't be bothered to repair. Every month even more back issues for the magazine archives arrived in boxes from the printer. They just sat lining the walls as no one could be bothered to carry them anywhere. At times, it was difficult just to get to the door at all.

The house was changing. Every now and then I would have to take a second look around, as I was sure that things looked different. I later discovered that inherited items of Victorian furniture would mysteriously disappear because they were being auctioned off for cash.

We had a bit of a cash problem now that my father was gone. There didn't seem to be a juicy life insurance policy to cash in, and the magazine revenues had dropped dramatically. I was at the stage of having to ask people on the Muswell Hill Broadway, the nearby shopping street, for a few pennies. I never saw it as begging, but I guess it was, as I was asking for money. But I really needed it, and my mum never seemed to have any. Any penny that entered the house was usually spent on more wine and spirits. So, without really thinking about it, I progressed to the art of selling the sweets.

The candies had to be worth something, so I set up a stall in front of the house, complete with a sign reading, "Sweets for Sale," and managed to sell some of them. My mother loved the idea, supporting me all the way, and even tried to get in more samples for me. I sold them much more successfully at school, naturally, and the practice paid off. I was now learning another very useful life skill, namely how to sell.

So one day when there was a knock on the door, I thought our visitor might be coming to buy some sweets. Normally the people who knocked at our door were bailiffs. The last time, a few weeks before, I slammed the door shut on two of them and ran upstairs, as I really didn't like bailiffs. I wasn't sure if I should answer it this time. Whoever it was must have been very small, as I couldn't see the silhouette of a head through the stained glass. Maybe it wasn't a person at all; could a London prankster have left a firecracker on our doorstep to blow up in our faces?

Eventually, inquisitiveness got the better of me. Bailiffs are tall, and besides, they would have been thumping on the door by then. So I felt compelled to answer it. But then I stopped myself again: What if someone really horrid was hiding at the side of the house, ready to jump me? I was too small to offer any form of defense. I was always wary about who was on our doorstep.

Finally, I summoned up some courage, slid the chain lock from the door, and opened it until the chain pulled tight. I peered through the gap. Curiously, the dogs hadn't barked when the doorbell went off. Peggy and Sheba waited behind me as I found myself facing this unexpected and truly miniature character. She was so small I looked right over the top of her head and into the night—you wouldn't have blamed me for not seeing anyone and shutting the door completely.

"Who are you?" I asked my new visitor, bending down to hold the dogs' collars but without losing eye contact.

"I have some news for you," she said.

This was some strange character, I thought. She looked like she had come straight off a film set, like she was over a hundred years old. Her face was engraved by deep folds. Every blemish and wrinkle could have told an ancient, handed-down fable. And I was in for a tale, too, one that I have never forgotten.

"What news is that, then?"

"Well, are you going to let me in or leave me here standing in the cold?" she said, holding her headscarf under her chin with her thumb and index finger to keep it in place.

"Who is it, Angus?" my mother shouted from within.

"Sorry, but who *are* you?" I asked.

"It doesn't matter who I am, but it does matter what I am going to say. Now, are you going to be a fine young man and get me a cup of tea and let me in? It's pretty cold standing here."

"Yes, okay, sure, come in." Before I had finished speaking, she had marched past the dogs and me, untying her headscarf and letting her long gray hair loose.

"Now then, where can we sit down? I have something to tell you."

She paused to take in the atmosphere, looked around the room, spotted the chocolate chip cookies near the couches, and headed straight for a place within a convenient arm's reach of the biscuits.

My mother called again from the top of the stairs.

"Everything okay?"

"Fine, it's just a lady with some news for us, that's all," I replied.

The lady made herself comfortable on the couch and patted the seat next to her, beckoning me to sit down.

"Would you like a cookie?"

"Thank you, young man," she said, grabbing one and then taking an impressively large bite considering her miniature size. "Something tragic has happened in this household," she noted, changing her tone to one much more emphatic. "I only come when terrible and great things happen. I feel a bit of both going on here."

She grabbed my hand and continued.

"There has been a terrible loss in this household, terrible for you and your family. But you . . ." she paused, placing the bony fingers of her other hand over the back of mine and focusing her beady eyes on me.

"You will be very lucky. Yes, a very lucky man indeed. You are going to go a long way in life. Look at you. Let me see your face so I remember you. A lot of people will know your name, all over the world. Oh yes, many, many people."

She paused again, gripping my hand tighter and closing her eyes for a moment.

"You will always have a lot of money, too." Then her eyes opened wide and she started laughing. "But you will never pass an exam in your life.

"I am told your life will be a 'sweet one.' You will have to work that one out for yourself. Tell me your name, I want to remember your name, as you are going to be a very well-known man later on. Many people will know who you are." Her eyes lit up and she added, "And sweet."

After I furnished this rather curious being with my name, she nodded and continued. At around ten years old, you don't really have any preconceptions about strange people who can predict the future turning up on your doorstep out of the blue. Even today, I still wonder about some of the things she said and if they will come true. And who was she, anyway? Amazingly, everything this person said *has* come true so far: the good luck, failing all my exams, the sweet life, and my path to becoming curiously well-known.

"But," she continued, "you will soon be going to America and Germany and . . ." Another dramatic pause, punctuated by her pushing the rest of the Scottish shortbread into her mouth, ". . . enjoy a sweet life, Angus."

How I was going to get to the US or Germany was beyond me. We had no money, the bailiffs were at the door, and I had never been much farther than the Isle of Wight or a Welsh bed and breakfast in Abergavenny, near the Brecon Beacons. There was no way we would be able to get to America. It was a distant place I knew about merely through pictures in magazines, the odd TV program, and photos of large cornfields in my essential schoolkids' atlas. And what of being well-known by many people, my life being sweet, and my trip to Germany?

The dogs were now somewhat bored, seeing she had no food to offer them, and I was left on the couch with nothing to say. I wanted to hear more. She squeezed my hand tighter.

"Yes, there's no way out, they will all know who you are," she said.

Well, that's perfectly cool, I thought, not really believing her.

Then she laughed and said, "But don't worry about the exams; you will never pass any."

I don't know why she found that bit so funny, as I am sure my mother wouldn't have liked that statement very much at all. "But have faith," she continued, "and your time will come. It's been terrible here, terrible for you all. But don't you ever give up. Be patient, for you are blessed."

She gave her message, looked at her watch, tied her scarf back up onto her head, and went back through the living room door, across the hallway, out the front door, and down the steps. I rushed over to the door to get another look, but she seemed to have vanished into thin air. How could someone walk down our front path that fast and then disappear completely? I ran onto the street, looking both ways. Who she was and where she came from, I shall never know.

Perhaps it was a dream, but whatever it was, she told me exactly what I needed to hear.

The dogs looked up at me and out onto the road, equally puzzled, until one of them noticed an unattended biscuit.

We often hear these stories, in which someone meets another person at a certain point in their life or bumps into someone on the street when they are about to make a good or very bad decision. It was one of those moments for me. It led to a decisive turning point in my life: I realized I would always *have* to be positive. It was the only way to go, as the other direction would involve a slow decline into my own personal darkness, where all sorts of creative goodies such as depression and drugs would be on offer.

It wasn't easy to see back then, but had this "meeting" not happened, I don't believe I would have become the impossibly positive person I am today. I would not have possessed the drive, ambition, and insane belief in achieving the impossible, such as becoming a TV personality, Britain's chief chocolate taster, and author.

But how on earth was I going to make it? I was recovering from the fire, a drugged-up mum, no money in the family, starvation, asphyxiation, schooling going down the drain, and now the added complication of no dad around. The difficulties continued for many years, decades even. I just got used to them, resulting in me becoming one of the most successful failures on the planet.

There are always better or worse off people, but not once have I ever stopped believing that I would make it, even when it seemed clear to everyone around me that I wouldn't succeed. I just keep saying yes when they say no. I try to say I *can* when they say I can't. And saying we *won't* when they say you *have* to, is so important. You can't listen to too many people's theories on success. It's your journey.

I have failed my way to success. Going out and being unlike everyone else, by relishing the fact that everyone says I am crazy, means I'm going to make it. That's the secret: Scribble when they say stop doodling, daydream when they say pay attention, and visualize your dream when they say be realistic. Imagine the impossible. Yes, you can even imagine that you can become the world's chief chocolate expert.

Some people say Colonel Sanders got hundreds of rejections before his Kentucky fried chicken was accepted. It's said that Edison went through ten thousand prototypes for his electric light bulb. Otto Frederick Rohwedder, the gentleman who invented the first bread slicing machine and subsequently the arrival of sliced bread, it's claimed, was a failure for fifteen years. Everyone said that he had the worst idea ever, and now it's the best idea, well, since sliced bread. Walt Disney was fired from his first job in the newspaper business, because apparently, he was not creative enough. As far as I can see, the only madness is staying the same person you were yesterday, without trying to be who you are meant to be today.

The strange character who visited our house that night and my father's spirit gave me hope, and from that day on I always wondered how on earth I would be "known all over the world" and how I would be so lucky.

My mother finally made it down the stairs while combing her hair at the same time; quite an athletic achievement this was for her, too.

"Who was it, Angus?"

"Mum, do you know anyone in America?"

"No, no one. Did I miss something?"

"Oh, I'm going to America and a country called Germany, and I will be very lucky, *and* I'm going to be famous, Mum. Yes, and it's all going to be sweet, very sweet. And . . . I'm not going to ever pass any exams."

"America? Now you really *are* joking, Angus. Where's the money going to come from for that?"

"I don't know," I replied, feeling a bit disappointed. "It was probably all rubbish, anyway."

My mother managed to pretend she was mildly interested for at least a minute or two, but predictably something more interesting won over talking about my future. She drifted off into the toxic current and disappeared into the kitchen.

And so the strange rendezvous with the "lady who spoke of the future," as I called her, was forgotten. That was until a few weeks passed and something fortuitous happened. Good things were rare, so I was ready for anything—even a fresh loaf of bread that wasn't stale would have been a minor miracle.

I was still struggling. My sister had gone to study history at Norwich University, and my brother, who is impossibly intelligent, sailed into one of the best schools in the country on a full scholarship.

Meanwhile, I hated school. I disagreed with everything that was asked of me, and everything required of me seemed pointless. I was always doubtful of what I was taught, anyway. I couldn't understand why my teachers thought a slide rule or knowing what a chalk scarp slope was could be vaguely interesting or useful, when I was struggling to stay alive and sane. In fact, I hated life, and I felt there was no hope or place for me.

I urgently needed something to keep me going, apart from sweets; even those were now left almost unattended. I let the dogs get the next few batches in the mail. My mother and I were in an inexorable decline. There seemed to be no way up and a lot further we could go down, but I persevered, saying to myself constantly that it *would* get better.

What on earth can happen now? I thought.

Soon after my father's passing I started asking what I believed to be a greater power than me. I lay in bed looking at a picture of my dad on my bedside table, asking in my head, *What next, Dad?* I had to believe in something, anything positive. Something had to happen or there was no point.

A few days passed, and one evening Mum came off the phone with an odd expression on her face. She had almost dropped it while looking right at me.

"Yeah, what?" I asked nonchalantly.

"It was your godmother on the phone," she answered slowly. "Angus, she lives in America with her husband and their son. What else did that lady say? Tell me, because she has asked me if you would like to go and stay in Vermont in the United States this coming summer for four months, all expenses paid."

I looked at her in complete disbelief, gauging how much she had had to drink, as I always did when she said something unusual; she did exaggerate brilliantly at the best of times. But a holiday where I might *not* be going to the Isle of Wight, to the same run-down campsite with nasty outside toilets with flies in them, result! Come on, you're having a laugh. A flight on a real jumbo jet, too? No way.

"Angus! What else did that lady say?" she shrieked. "You are going to America, all paid for. And that's not all, there's more. Sit down, I have been thinking. I know it's been really tough, so in the meantime I have been planning for you to come to Germany with me to the big confectionery and sweets show. It's the biggest confectionery event in the world."

She leaned over and gave me a hug.

"I'm so sorry," she said.

There were times when she realized what she had become, namely something she clearly didn't want to be. My mother really did love me, and there were welcome patches of a real mum emerging at intervals.

So now I was going to America. I was going to get a tour of the whole of the United States in an old Volvo with a relation I never even knew existed. But first I was off to Germany. Hope started to seep in at last.

It all came true. I have never passed an exam in my life, but I have had good luck and money in my account, and it's always been, well, sweet. All but one of her predictions have come true. I still wonder about her saying that all will know my name. Am I really going to be famous? Who knows?

The good luck prediction was particularly accurate; I have been very lucky. Some would say that I have been unlucky, but I have been lucky enough to see that the bad luck leads me to the celebrations. That's being lucky, simple as that. It's how you see yourself.

I needed all the luck I could get. I was going to start at senior school soon after my trip to Germany, and my mother could hardly afford the uniform, but I had another plan. I was going to find all the sweets a young boy could *ever* get his hands on, ever. Here I was, getting ready to go on a private tour around a confectionery trade show (the biggest in the world), and then, to top it all, I was off to the US.

The plan was for me to attend a trade show where I could explore one thousand stands set up by the world's leading international producers of biscuits, bubble gums, chews, cakes, chocolates, and snacks. I ran upstairs right away to find an empty case from the attic. I wasn't packing anything—it was coming back filled with the largest, most shameless hoard of sweets of all time. My Willy Wonka training was proceeding full steam ahead.

The private doors of an industry were opening for me. I was one of the very few kids to attend the show, because strictly speaking, kids were not really allowed to be there. My mother arranged for me to take time off school, and I took a week off to attend the University of Sweets. And what a magnificent adventure it was to be.

I had endless questions: "Does it snow in Germany? What are the trees like there? What do I say if I meet someone from Germany, Mum?"

I looked out the window admiring the Ford Cortina XL and focused on a particularly comforting sight—the large trunk. That was all that mattered to me; it was soon going to be unforgivably rammed full of delicious empty carbs.

CHAPTER 5

Welcome to the World of Confectionery

The trade show ISM, which is short for the Internationale Süßwaren-messe, meaning international sweets show, was *the* place where just about all independent confectionery companies from around the world "internationalized" their sales and started exports. It was 1974 and my first trip to a show where many of the UK confectionery businesses, such as Tunnock's (tea cakes), Walker's Nonsuch (toffees), and Walkers (shortbread), boosted their trade exports and in many cases started from scratch. Up until then, few companies exported.

The show, like many German trade shows, was started after World War II to encourage trade and investment in the country. They did a fine job, too; in fact, many of the leading trade shows continue to take place in Germany today. The print industry's drupa, for example, encompasses a huge almost 500,000 square feet space; the event is the largest of its kind. Germany also hosts gigantic shows for everything from bodybuilding to dentistry to fine foods and wines. Other shows in Europe have managed to compete with them, but the German govern-ment still supports the companies with export agencies. Over here in the UK, it's fight for yourself. I run my own show and exhibition called the London Chocolate Forum every year in the London Docklands, and the government gives me absolutely zero help, even though 90 percent of my company turnover is from overseas. There used to be grants, export organizations, and help for UK companies wishing to export, but I believe most assistance has dried up.

I was busy getting ready for action for my trip to Germany's ISM, so I made myself look older and more important for the occasion. I even bought a hideous green velvet jacket, which I thought was sublimely cool, and thought it was a great idea to cut my own hair: big mistake number two. I'm not sure if it was better than my mother's pudding bowl–style cuts, but at least I had done *something* to prepare for my trip.

With the remains of my pocket money, I had also purchased a Vivitar instamatic camera with a marvel of the new technology of the 1970s—a *built-in flash* that was powered by a battery. I called myself the *Kennedy's* photographer, and even though I had a film cartridge that could take just twelve lousy photos for the whole week, I was *the* magazine photographer. It even said so on my press badge.

My pocket Vivitar was one of those annoying cameras that, despite the viewfinder, always managed to chop someone's head off when you got the prints back from the printer. Even when I did get the head in the frame, the shots were hopelessly out of focus, smudged, and colorless. Nonetheless, I had a press badge to pin to my hideous green suit, I had a job title, and I felt important, especially with my homemade, wonky, and totally hideous haircut.

As we had no money for the trip, we would either camp or stay in very cheap hotels, the type that are very close to airports and at the end of the runways with a curtain to divide the rooms. As we walked into the exhibition halls in Cologne, we passed the luxury hotels where the rich and successful businesspeople would stay, something I could only dream of at the time. As my mother and I walked past one of the buildings, the Maritim, I said to her, "One day, Mum, we'll be here in the best hotel in Cologne, you and I together."

I vowed then to make it happen, and sure enough, not long before her death, I managed to book her into that hotel. By that time, she was reduced to a wheelchair, and it was extremely difficult to get her around the city. However, I did it and it made her happy, so no regrets.

And so, one early morning in late January, my mother and I got into the car and caught the ferry from Dover across the English Channel.

Once in Germany and throughout the entire drive to Cologne, I looked for snow on the ground, searching every field and rooftop, but sadly nothing. How odd, Germany looked like the UK. (But we never had much snow in London.) While all my classmates were plowing through their school math books and calculating how many sweets were left in a bag after Jill took five, John nineteen, and Phil six, I was going to take the real sweets out of the bag all for myself. I was going to take so many that no one would be able to count them—and directly from the people who made them, too.

Mum managed to not drink for the drive to Cologne, which was an unexpected treat, too, so yet again I was pleased that I had survived another clear suicide mission. As we were travelling on the autobahn, I asked her straight out what happened to her when she was young and what her life was like back then. You don't just suddenly drink like she did. There is nearly always some reason why. I had my suspicions; even at ten years old you can work things out. I suspected that she was drinking to hide pain or abuse. I couldn't believe what she finally told me.

When she was ten, during World War II, my mother was sent to Canada. Around two million British children were evacuated and taken from their families (with their parents' permission) to so-called safer countries. It was called Operation Pied Piper and carried out like a military maneuver without an understanding of the huge psychological damage it would inflict upon the children who left their parents and boarded trains with just a small bag and no idea where they were going. Like many children who were sent away at that time, when she arrived in another country, she was almost immediately bullied and alienated. She told me the story of a boy in her new class in Vancouver who tormented her, day in and day out.

This boy was the school thug and he welcomed her arrival. She was different and spoke with a strange English accent, so he had good reason to single her out. He eventually managed to move his place in the classroom so his desk was positioned directly behind hers. He would sit behind her and call her names. This continued for weeks.

She managed to ignore his insults, so he upped his game. During the following weeks, halfway through a lesson, he would stick a compass into her back so he could make her scream out loud in the class; that always made him laugh.

Outside the classroom was no better. She was teased for her English accent and was never left alone. This continued for months, and the family that she was with offered little support.

She had no explanation as to why she had been sent away, when the likelihood of her house in the country being bombed was desperately remote. Her whole life had been turned upside down in an instant. One day she was a happy little girl in a small village near Berkhamsted, blessed with her friends, a brother, and parents, and the next she found herself in the middle of Vancouver, far away from her family, being tormented daily and made to do chores around an unfamiliar house. Her brother was not sent away, due to his illness, and she never forgave her parents.

When she could no longer put up with the bully, she plotted her revenge. She told me that it got to the point that it was him or her, and she *had* to do something. My mother was, right up until she died, a formidable character. I think she certainly learned from what she did.

One evening, after another compass episode and with blood-stains on the back of her school blouse, she waited for her moment. She knew the boy would be near the playground waiting for her after school, but this time she would be ready. She left the building through another doorway at the back of the school, where she had a little "treat" waiting for him.

He was waiting for her, itching to start his tirade of insults, but he didn't know that *she* was approaching *him* from behind, and that she had brought a plank with her and laid it by the school wall near where he always waited. To her horror, he turned around and saw her, so she couldn't pick up the wood.

He started his taunts, looking for appreciation from his gang at his skills in teasing and belittling. Soon it was finished and he turned his back on her, laughing, and walked away, probably feeling satisfied that he'd done enough damage for the day.

To the amazement of the other schoolchildren, my mother picked up the piece of wood, approached him from behind, and swung it as hard as she could, striking him on the back of his head. He went down without a word, to a spellbound silence. The English "Pom," as English people were referred to at the time, had fought back. He was taken, she said, presumably to the hospital, and she never saw him again. She was always an advocate for standing up to everyone and taught me to do the same. "Never, ever let anyone bully you," she would say, "*never!*" There are bullies of all ages; most of them aren't kids.

No one ever touched her after the plank episode, but the damage had been done. It wasn't the bullying, she told me, it was the fact that she had been sent away. How could her parents do it? Children were sent away in case their homes were bombed, but her family lived in the country. Not a single bomb would ever drop near her house, and her elder brother wasn't sent with her.

I am pleased she told me her story, and as I said before I never blame anyone for their drinking because there is always a reason behind it, but it was all taking its toll on her, and her master, the drink, would eventually win.

After she told me her story I thought about how we had never planned to get into the mess we were in, to have an about-to-be-repossessed house in North London, but we made the most of it all—a house full of candy, rotten food, mice, and various other parasites with which I shared my bedroom. I wondered if I would ever have a happy mum, a clean bedroom, a normal life, or a uniform that resembled anything like what my friends were wearing, but now I could cheer myself up, knowing that I knew her secret, and also that I was about to be the first to try the world's latest candy concoctions. I was soon to be just about the only child to be allowed into the world's biggest confectionery show.

———————

As we walked around the exhibition hall, I watched my mother in action. To my surprise, everyone adored her, calling her name out from every stand—she was in hot demand. She was a real people's editor. Her memory was impeccable, and she rattled off facts and figures about everyone's business and the industry with ease. It was impressive. She was the most brilliant character there, the woman of the show. They absolutely loved her, especially the boldness in her appearance and what she said. She never wore makeup—ever—and walked around barefoot while all the other women made great efforts to look good. She seemed to come alive at the show and be in her element. Magazines thrive on character editors, and that's how

I run mine today. People buy people. Some knew she had a drinking problem, but mostly they were unaware.

She knew everyone, and I was taken by it. Everywhere she went, I went. I was learning all the time and being introduced to the top people in the industry at every opportunity. I moved from country to country, talking to companies from Greece, the United States, Brazil, Canada, and Australia. She knew them all, and at last I had the chance to see my mother's other life.

My job at the show was to look important when I clearly wasn't (that's what most people do in business anyway), and to take photos of these wonderful people and their fine products. They were the characters who owned the confectionery businesses. There were many more family businesses than there are today; it wasn't until the early 1980s that a huge number of takeovers began to change the landscape of the industry.

Finally all those sweets in jars and on the shelves of my local corner shop had meaning. I saw Callard and Bowser butterscotch, Walker's Nonsuch toffees, Fry's Chocolate Cream, Maynards wine gums, Paynes Poppets, Cadbury, Black Jacks, Humbugs, Flying Saucers, and lots of other products of the time, some of which are still available today. They were all made by the wonderful people at this gigantic show.

The families who owned the businesses were still involved then, even the Cadbury family, whom I met on one occasion. Many producers are history now, and the brands are owned by huge groups or have disappeared completely. In the 1960s in the United Kingdom alone, there were around three thousand confectionery producers; today it's estimated there are a few more than three hundred. The big companies just get bigger and bigger. Nestlé is now the biggest food company in the world.

It's the same for the machinery and ingredients groups that supply the industry. It's a problem for publishing because over the last twenty years, what was once an advertising base of five hundred companies has withered down to around 250. There are fewer companies and fewer people employed to actually read the magazines, too. For example, just a handful of companies dominate the UK industry, while in the US, it's reported, Hershey's controls a sizable chunk of the market.

Advertising in the 1980s was published in amazing volumes; whole printed directories with hundreds of pages of advertising used to exist. Publishing was booming, as anyone in the industry will tell you about the "golden times," but it's very different now. You have to be smart to remain in the game, with either a strong presence on the Web or at events. Most magazines cannot survive on their own, so most publishers produce a few magazines together for the company to survive. Sometimes I feel like I have one of the few publishing companies still surviving that publishes a single monthly magazine.

The people I met at that show were the real Willy Wonkas, not me. There were, and are still, thousands of them around the world. My mother did business with the parents, and now their children are my customers. (I first met some of those children, also secretly smuggled in, at that show. It's quite an incestuous industry, really.) I know a lot of lovely people in the industry who would never sell their companies, and I am so pleased they didn't give in. They exhibit their confections on their stands, aisle after aisle at the trade shows, all over the world from Dubai to China, year after year, selling their amazing new products.

There are many confectioners that either call themselves "Willy Wonkas" or the press does. Why people think it should require the skills of a weird man with a hat and a purple suit, who harms children, to make magical sweets is beyond me. The original Willy Wonka broke every health and safety regulation with his daft clothing, just walking round the factory. And what exactly is a Willy Wonka anyway? I think it's something we want to believe in when so many of us lead such predictable lives. I personally don't have a sweets factory, I'm not single, and I love my children (and all kids for that matter), so I'm nothing like the fictional Willy Wonka, thank God! But as you know by now, even though I'm not a candy maker, I still get called a Willy Wonka and even from time to time call myself one. For me though, it's all in the name of good fun!

All week, I was handed sweets to sample right from the owners' hands: Tunnock's tea cakes from Mr. Tunnock, Swizzels Love Hearts from Mr. Matlow, and Walkers shortbread from Mr. Walker. Then they'd ask what I thought of their range (while my mouth was still stuffed with goodies), and they took a genuine interest in my somewhat fresh, young opinion.

Many had children of their own, so they would ask me why I was at the show and not at school, in which case I would rush to take a photo with my camera (well, pretend to) and change the subject. Luckily, I was saved as the camera made a click and the flash went off, so it looked like I was taking a photo. They all seemed satisfied with my pointless work.

"I can't keep up with it, all this modern technology," some would say.

"Angus, I never knew they could make cameras that size," others would muse.

Of course, it was hardly a camera. I was a bit of a fake, and they were being kind, but I was there and feeling important and receiving copious amounts of free sweets, so who cared?

Each time we met a candy producer, I would carefully point at an interesting new product on display on their stands and ask if I could have a sample to take home. They always obliged. I was now getting myself a real booty, a hoard of chocolates that would set me up beautifully for when I went back to school. I even managed to get my hands on some of the first single-origin chocolate, which we seem to think is a new invention but like most things has been around for years.

In the UK at the time, chocolate tended to come in either the milk or the plain (dark) variety—as opposed to today, when we can choose where the beans come from, how they are sourced, how much cocoa or sugar they contain, and even the processing temperature. The word *plain* has been dropped since, as it didn't sound very attractive. I managed to get my hands on chocolates labeled with different cocoa percentages, for example a bar saying 63 percent cocoa. A product that wasn't a milk or a dark chocolate was unheard of at that time. And then I was handed a box of real Turkish delights (from Greece), which came hidden in icing sugar, packed in beautiful brass-hinged wooden boxes and wax paper—a product that was not a rose-flavored gelatin, cellophane-wrapped countline enrobed in chocolate.

When I took the ferry back to Britain, my bags were filled with amazing and unusual sweets from all over the world. It was with these novelties that I would start refining my skills down to an art. Chocolate and candy were my new currency, and my knowledge of the confectionery industry was boosted considerably by my weeklong intensive training course. As we were press, we were told everything about the products, and I sat in on all the interviews with my mother as she worked, taking notes, listening, and watching.

Listening and watching are the most important skills for a journalist to learn, and my mother was magnificent at both. Sometimes you collect material for your stories years before you write them; for example, I met Mr. Boyd Tunnock when I was twelve and I wrote an article on him thirty years later.

The wise know when *not* to speak. Being quiet is a type of learning, I guess. It takes skill not to speak.

My mother had a wonderful way of getting people to talk. She was extremely clever and somehow managed to remember the facts she acquired at these shows as opposed to more practical domestic matters, and they all loved her. I also managed to steer her off the drink when we were away, which helped enormously. When she put her mind to it, she was a very good writer, too. My job was to make sure people didn't see the real problems she faced every morning. I had to keep her alive and looking okay, especially because I needed to get my super booty back to England. We made a good team and somehow kept the business going together.

She knew she wouldn't last too long in this world, and she had clearly decided it was time to teach me all she could manage and introduce me to everyone she knew. Even though she was mildly drunk throughout most of the day, no one really noticed. We pulled off a beautiful subterfuge with a certain amount of panache. From then on, I supported her right to her deathbed, when she and I agreed that it was "time to go."

The week passed quickly. I was sad to leave the bridge over the Rhine River and the spectacular view of the centuries-old, five-hundred-foot-tall Cologne Cathedral. Little did I know I would see it every year, every January.

The car was laden with goodies, and my trading enterprise was about to flourish. I had no idea how much the kids at school would trade to get their hands on my newly found and not-on-the-market-yet booty, but it was safe to say that I was never going to be a normal kid.

I had become the odd, quiet character who would disappear from school for weeks, survive another awful trauma, and come bouncing back from magical places with unusual candies and news of trips and people from faraway lands. Somehow, I was the happiest person who could have been be so sad.

After our return from Cologne, my mother made the preparations to get me back to school again. What on earth would they say this time?

CHAPTER 6

The Candy Kid Goes Back to School

As I prepared to go back to school, my mind was on the future. I couldn't believe that the following summer, just after my eleventh birthday, I would be plucked from my home and flown off to the United States. Germany was far enough, but the US seemed like a faraway galaxy.

The US today is one of my favorite places to visit, not least because Americans are the biggest consumers of chocolate on the planet. Actually, the US chocolate market is worth $21.6 billion and accounts for 28 percent of the entire chocolate market. And it's set to get bigger because, I heard at a conference, as humans we are creating a city the size of New York every month in terms of people being born. The global population is reported to be on track to grow to more than nine billion people by 2050.

Food producers, it's widely reported, are going to have to produce more food in the next forty years than the total of what was produced in the last eight hundred years. And chocolate alone is a serious business: it's already worth a cool $75 billion a year worldwide, and we are eating more and more.

So once again, I was dropped off at school, albeit in a new classroom with some new classmates, who experienced another random, unexpected appearance of the candy kid.

I guessed that I had to attend a new class as I had lost so much work time. I looked shabby and felt completely ill prepared for my first day back, and worried about how I would be received by the new kids.

First impressions are everything. I felt like a plain buffoon, complete with a haircut administered by my mum—aligned with my own personal modifications—pudding-bowl style. It made me look like a miniature French monk from the sixteenth century. I was going to be crucified.

I wished I could have boarded the jumbo and gone straight to the Boston airport. I was so nervous I almost didn't get on the bus, but in the end, I armed myself with a box of my original Turkish delights (from Greece) and set off.

The bus journey to my school in Camden Town from Muswell Hill was torturous. The best thing about it was the amazing pet shop that sold tarantulas, which I dived into when all my friends rammed themselves into the sweetshop during the wait. There were never any downstairs seats on the bus, so I used to go to the upper deck, which we called "the gas chamber." There was so much cigarette smoke up there that you couldn't even see a seat, let alone get lucky enough to sit on one. I hated going on the bus, but finding a window seat meant that for a good forty-five minutes I could almost breathe.

On my first ride back to school I finally found a seat when someone got off at Kentish Town, and I sat next to a rather hideous character with fingers yellowed from years of nicotine. I saw his bony, angular fingers shaking slightly with a cigarette stuck in between them as he let the smoke coil up to my face. Even when I waved my hands in front of him to send the smoke back, it made no difference. There were many like him staring out the window at nothing in particular, quietly smoking their way to an early funeral. I reached for a Turkish delight to calm my nerves.

It was one of the posh packets that come in a small wooden box, with the cubed jellies buried in a good inch or so of icing sugar. The icing goes everywhere when you attempt to excavate one out of the pack. I didn't notice that my blazer was gradually collecting an even covering of the white dust during the journey. Icing sugar on a dark blue blazer shows up brilliantly, which is especially good for your first day back at school when you want to blend in with the other dark blue blazers. The sugar was finely coated over my black leather shoes, too, so for my debut I looked like I had stepped straight out of a jelly factory's starch molding department.

The school must have known about my rather desperate home situation, because I had, rather unusually, an appointment with the headmaster on my first day back. I had no idea why I had to see him, and it merely added to my collection of wandering nerves, which were accumulating as quickly as the icing sugar on my blazer. When I walked into the headmaster's office, the first thing I spotted was a grand collection of drinks on his walnut side cabinet—all decanted into fine crystal jugs.

In those days, professionals were open about their drinking. He had a large crystal tumbler of Scotch whisky on his mahogany desk, resting close to his trembling fingers, and by looking at his nose, which was very swollen and covered in burst red blood vessels under the skin, I knew right away he had a drinking problem. I could spot the signs a mile off.

The headmaster was also known for his fiery temper, which one or two other children had conveniently informed me about before my meeting. I realized when I saw him that it was caused by drinking, and that any anger he might show was not necessarily being directed at me. I had seen it all before. I figured he might forget he was even angry and nod off to sleep.

Oh Christ, not another drinker, I thought. Another person in my life who drinks this stuff; that was all I needed. I stood in his office while he remained somewhat beached behind his desk. He was so large, it was hardly surprising that he made no effort to stand up and shake my hand. He didn't do anything to make me feel even mildly at ease. He finally reached for his glass for a gulp, which was obviously the main purpose of his morning. At that moment, two small dogs leaped out from under his desk. They took great interest in my shoes, and started immediately to lick the icing sugar off.

"We don't really allow sweets in the school, Master Kennedy," he said.

He seemed to stress the word *really* as his pets continued to lap the sugar off my black shoes. I was already becoming an exception to one of his rules. He found my appearance particularly amusing. I knew it didn't matter *what* he thought, as looking at the state he was in, he wouldn't remember much of what he had seen and said anyway.

"But you seem to be the perfect walking, edible candy already, Kennedy." He roared with laughter, amusing himself considerably. "Even my dogs want to eat you," he continued, almost allowing the sacred tumbler to slip from his hand and bounce off his belly.

He was clearly overdoing it somewhat, surprising himself at what he thought to be such wit from his pickled tongue. In retrospect, I think he was trying to be affectionate. He knew what had happened to me with my father passing, and I guessed this was his way to be friendly, in between waking up to reality, here and there. But there wasn't much brain left for me to be friendly with. I had seen it all before. After what I had been through, I didn't really care much what he said.

He seemed a little put out by the fact that his domineering lines didn't affect me as I reached down to stroke his dogs. I looked at him from the corner of my eye as he quickly gulped down another whisky while he thought I couldn't see him.

I should offer him something to go with it, I thought. I paused and then couldn't resist.

"Turkish delight, sir?" I asked. "I know they are not allowed, but . . ."

I reached out my arm, the box balanced on my palm, and opened the lid, to the delight of his dogs, who were now furiously licking the carpet.

His bushy eyebrows were the first to react; they rose so high they almost touched his greasy black hair. In an instant, they returned with equal speed to their usual ugly position, as his intoxicated brain strained with the welcome offer from a mere schoolboy.

"Don't mind if I do, Kennedy," he said as he took a long pause for breath. "One of my favorites. And the real ones, too, Kennedy, none of that cellophane-wrapped kiddies' stuff. These are real Turkish delights, Kennedy, you have the *real* thing. Now, where did you get these, ancient Greece or something?"

I decided I actually quite liked him. He was a friendly old goat and, like my mother, he probably had his reasons for his ways. I walked over to his desk with his terriers now leaping up at me for a bigger prize—a whole jelly.

"Thank you, Kennedy," he said as his sausage fingers grabbed a pink square of jelly, leaving a trail of sugar on his desk. "Do let me know if you are okay," he said as he pushed the melting jelly onto his tongue. "Come back tomorrow, same time."

There's a real man there, somewhere, I thought. That's the trick. My sweets were working just fine—as they always had done and always would do.

I still use candy to my advantage now. I will call a newspaper and ask if they'd like to do a story on chocolate, and the journalist will say, "Well, not really." And I will then say I can set up a free private tasting of the latest chocolates from around the world, and they're round like a shot.

"You will tell me, Kennedy, if you are down, won't you?"

"Yes, sir," I replied, standing up straight and almost saluting him with respect. "Yes, sir, I will."

I closed the wooden lid on the box, sending a new storm cloud of sugar particles into the air, a descending cloud formed over the delighted terriers' heads as they jumped and licked the air. He called me again.

"Kennedy, bribery will get you everywhere," he said. "See you again soon."

By this time, he seemed to have exhausted perhaps a little too much energy for that time of day. He retreated into his leather chair as his fingers curled themselves around his tumbler once again. I returned to my new classroom and was welcomed by a round of giggles from kids who had noticed the most amusing sight of the year: the boy covered in sugar.

How sweet.

The first thing I noticed about the new geometry teacher who greeted me was that he wasn't wearing shoes. His curly brown hair was so long I could hardly see his eyes.

"Cool," he said, admiring the icing sugar on my blazer. "Go and sit down over there," he continued, pointing to my new desk.

I sat down rather rigidly for the rest of the morning, wondering how break time would go.

A trip to the headmaster was always associated with children coming back crying, and there seemed to be a certain amount of confusion as to why I wasn't looking deeply upset about the experience and, moreover, why I was covered in trails of candy dust. There was a curiosity about my existence in my new classroom. The questions were being asked already: Why was I not crying after visiting the headmaster? Why did I look like a monk, smell like a used cigarette stub from the bus journey, and appear to be coated in icing sugar?

School was not at the top of my agenda; besides, I had not long ago been told I wouldn't pass any exams, anyway. The good news was that my new desk, where I was to spend the rest of the year, was right by the window, so most of the time I could gaze beyond my immediate surroundings and dream and wonder about real life outside the classroom. I used to watch people passing by the window all the time, wondering what they were doing, where they were walking to, and why. What did *they* learn at school? Are they using their knowledge now? Was it equally as useless as it seemed to me? I always was a bit of a dreamer. In my opinion, it takes a childhood to learn things at school and then a lifetime to unlearn it all.

But tragedies teach you to think differently. I wanted answers to my life, answers I knew my teachers, with all the goodwill in the world, may not be able to provide, and certainly answers for which they didn't have the time to provide.

When someone taught about the angles of an isosceles triangle and seemed to present it as such vital knowledge, I didn't get it. I felt alienated and that I was being pumped through a system. I wondered about real things happening to me, how my mum was coping at home, and if I would have to pick her up from the floor in the evening. More importantly, my mind was occupied by what I could swap for my new 63 percent cocoa single-origin Ecuadorian solid chocolate bar.

I had seen her before in the junior school and couldn't believe my luck when I discovered that Lily, on whom I had an inescapable crush, was now in my math class. I started thinking really hard about how I could get her attention and subsequently paid no attention to the teacher. So that handsomely put an end to my learning math, not that I was equipped to learn it anyway. I just could not take my eyes off her. I was entirely overcome by her very existence in every way possible. When she walked past me, I was so obsessed with her presence that even the smell of her soap made me melt in the school corridor. As is typical with so many school crushes, I entered an almost panic-stricken state when I came anywhere near her.

The boy next to me in geometry had resigned himself to the fact that he was now sitting next to the weirdo, the one with the pudding-bowl haircut and a sugary jumper. Whether we liked it or not, I was going to have to share half my working life with this individual, so we had to make an effort. I lifted the lid of my desk to reveal my priceless chocolate bar that I had hidden, offered him a piece, and immediately had his attention.

I wanted to ask him about my new sweetheart in the corner, to see if she had any boyfriends. But the hippie-haired teacher started waffling on about angles and looking my way. I didn't mind geometry though, as it seemed to be connected to the stars in some way. That was the only reason I managed to retain interest. I always believed that one of those stars (Arcturus or the Pleiades) up there was mine and it was guiding me to freedom. I still do.

"What's your name?" I asked him while sliding the chocolate his way and across the desk.

"Gary," he whispered through the corner of his lips, his hand over his mouth.

He was well dressed, though his shirt was a strange color: white. Mine were mostly blue or a tint of red from going through the laundry with all the other clothes. All my other classmates had been to the barber, too, to get their hair done, and above all they seemed to be interested in what the teacher was preaching. How on earth was I going to survive all this and be like them?

"It's break time in ten minutes; meet you over by the witch's hat in the playground," Gary said.

The witch's hat was a cone-shaped iron-frame contraption that you could jump on and spin around while it made the most terrible creaking noise, as it was never oiled or checked. The trick was to avoid getting your legs caught underneath, or they could be broken. The school had no playground, so we all went two-by-two to the grounds across the road in Regent's Park, next to London Zoo. I could see the playground from my window in the classroom and still today, the feeling of wanting to escape from the lessons and go play there is etched into my soul.

"Great, see you there," I said.

No one really wanted to talk to the weirdo at break time. It was a relatively new class and we were all trying in some way to prove ourselves. But I was badly dressed, and too unusual for any further contact. Gary was a good kid, and the chocolate helped, but it wasn't cool to talk to the new arrivals without knowing who they were. Nevertheless, I was about to be thrown into the great testing ground, to see if I was in or out. It was an apparent test of the mind, body, and soul of a boy: the football pitch.

"Come on," said Gary, "you can be on my team."

My heart lifted, and we ran over to the pitch to meet the other boys, who were showing off by spinning balls on their heads and on various other limbs, or at least pretending to.

"This is Angus. He's on my team," announced Gary as he raised my arm.

I was tall and well built; they imagined I was a great player. The pitch was my test to discover, from that day on until the last day of term, amen, whether I was a reject or not, no in-betweens.

That's the way school was, and I guess it still is in many ways. I looked at the side of the pitch, and a row of recently manufactured football dropouts looked on at the Great Test of Angus Kennedy. This was the school's way of testing the boys: a lousy game of football. My future and my fate were in the making.

After my first ten years of life, I guess I held a certain amount of maturity, which I imagine might have made me seem a little distant. I hated football and cricket and couldn't see the point in either of them. I loved running and swimming, and for some reason I was particularly fast at the former, so I duly went onto the football pitch to join my team, to be crowned the hero of the day.

Then I spotted Lily, who had come over to watch. My heart raced, and my legs crumpled. The girl I had such a crush on was there at the side of the pitch, watching me. This was my time. The best day of my life was in the making, a day that would make up for all the bad days of the past. How proud my mother would be of me! All I needed to do was to score a goal. There was such a thing as justice in life after all, and finally it would be mine.

Lily looked even more beautiful than she did in the classroom as she stood holding the top of her coat closed to the cold air. That's the problem with crushes, you just set like jelly in a worse state every time they appear. The whistle went, and in an instant I was part of a chaotic moving clump of twenty or so kids all running at the ball at the same time for a few unplanned minutes. I was fast on my feet, and at last the ball was booted right out from our clump to the other end of the pitch, thereby presenting my chance to impress.

I found myself on my own and first to the ball with considerable ease. My speed had surprised even the unexcited teacher on duty, who was now drawing on his last cigarette and standing beside the pitch before blowing the whistle to end the fun and start lessons.

All I had to do was pop the ball in and then later offer Lily the rest of my very best chocolate from a country I couldn't pronounce—an easy job. The goalkeeper and me, no problem. I eyed up the goal and prepared to shoot. I snatched a last look over my shoulder at my sweet love-to-be. This was it, I was going to win her, too. I kicked hard and prayed.

Please go in, just one good thing this whole year, Mr. God, and that's it, my only request, and I will never ask again for anything till next year, promise.

The ball went sailing beautifully through the air, but, to my eternal horror, it not only missed, but it landed and twisted wildly over the grass and came to a miserable, damp halt near the corner flag. It was a truly spectacular miss.

My grand initiation test was over. The rather sad row of boys moved up at the edge of the pitch to prepare a place for the new dropout. Lily walked away with her friends. The whistle sounded, the duty teacher stubbed out his cigarette on the grass, and I left the pitch.

I walked as far away as possible and sat by the large conker tree (otherwise known as a horse chestnut) next to the playground, where another group of kids was looking for conkers, or what were known to us kids as "cheese slicers," on the ground. Why was life so cruel? I felt outcast and alienated as I watched the football stars walking away with the girls, laughing as they relived every detail of my terrible shot.

What now? I couldn't even get in with the exam swots, the club of kids who got excited over being tested. I sat alone against the horse chestnut tree.

School until this moment, I thought, could have been my window to the real world, where I could make friends with normal people, meet kids with money, and see nice gardens with amazing climbing frames. School was my passport to clean houses, lots of interesting toys, and delicious cooking. My chance had melted as if it had never been offered.

I reached into my blazer pocket for my last Turkish delight, wondering who invented that cruel game, football. How many other young kids had fallen to the ground when they missed? My first day back at a new school after the holidays was a disaster. Gary came over and stood opposite me, out of breath from running.

"Don't worry, you get another chance, Angus. The next test is cricket."

My heart sank as I held the candy box in my hand. It was really over now, surely, game set, and match; I hated cricket, too. Now I had given up, and with that I reached for a last cube of jelly.

"Cool, what's that?" asked Gary.

"Oh, it's a *real* Turkish delight. They don't all have to be covered in chocolate and come in a shiny purple wrapper. They don't have to come from Turkey either. These came from Greece. They're flavored with rose hip. They originated from Turkey but also from the Middle East. Turkish delights were made over two hundred fifty years ago, you know? The Sultan of Turkey was mad on them. Did you know it's the oldest confectionery in the world? The ones you are thinking of and that you eat probably come from a factory up north. I went there, you know? But these are really special ones. You can't buy these in England. I got these from a friend in Cologne last week at a giant show with one thousand candy companies. Sweets everywhere. They come from a friend of the family in Greece. We got loads. Listen, I have to go, Gary."

I got up and walked over to the park gates. I didn't want to know what he thought, as they were my sweets and that was all I had. That was all I ever had. It was over for me. I walked home that evening to save the bus fare.

"How was school, Angus?" my mother asked.

"Yeah, fine," I replied as cheerily as I could muster.

However, my stomach tightened. I was really dreading the next day. I went up to my room and felt so alone. My only chance to experience a sense of normal life and friends was over. I tried hard to have faith in what my fortune said, but I dived onto my bed, bracing myself for more tests to alienate me even further the next day.

My mother knew something was up. Perhaps she had been saving this one for me; I shall never know.

"Angus, I have something here for you," she shouted up the stairs. "It's a kind of exploding sweet called strawberry popping candy. It explodes in your mouth, really. Quickly, come down and try it. Do you want some for your school snack for tomorrow?"

Popping candy? I was interested. I went downstairs with the dogs, who were equally keen to try some and possibly even witness my mother exploding in front of them. Without my realizing it, my career had started in earnest. Someone I had met in Cologne had sent me this crazy exploding candy in small packets and asked me to test it on the kids at school.

I was definitely going to take it to school the next day and win people over. Curiously I was taking product to an audience and seeking opinion. That's exactly what an editor like me today does. And so it came to be that my Wonka career officially began. Candy was part of my life in every way.

I couldn't wait to get to school, and the reaction was predictably frenzied. Perhaps there was a chance after all to win Lily over with some popping candy. The kids immediately formed a circle around me during the school break and begged me to let them try some of the magic exploding granules, holding out their hands, jumping up and down, and screaming, "me, me, me," like a perfect chorus of Russian circus seals. At last I was carving my way up the social ladder, but it wasn't to be.

The new senior school had different plans. I was to be *educated* and prepared for the school's first run of entrance exams. I didn't think it was possible for me to pass anything. The fortune teller's words started coming true, as they'd continue to be, apart from the driving test, which I believe is the only test I have ever actually passed.

And so the next stage of life kicked in: my great string of academic failures. The mini-Wonka was going to now have to learn how to fail his way to success. My motto is still, "I learn what I experience and forget what I am taught."

I continued to take my weird and wacky products to the new senior school and try to find a way somehow to edge closer to Lily, but of course it was not the purpose of a school to be a giant candy testing ground, and the teachers were getting wind of my growing popularity. The kids in school realized what I was about after they went wild over the popping candy. A few kids were even fighting in the school corridors to get ahold of some. It did the trick and lifted my spirits once again, which I so desperately needed.

Eventually the teachers had pretty much forgotten about my troubles at home, and anyway, they were paid to help me pass exams and gain entrance to the next school. Gradually over the months, my school changed from being a friendly place where you met other kids, played, and enjoyed the day, to an environment in which you had to pass memory tests to look good and wade through ridiculous amounts of homework every night.

I am still against homework, even now that I have kids. They always ask for help, and with five kids, we find ourselves helping them with hours of homework every night, often with them crying over the kitchen table saying they can't do it while Mum and Dad are reaching for another glass of chardonnay. If I had a few million, the first thing I would do would be to buy a school, have an assembly, and announce right away that all homework is *banned*!

Curiously, my sixteen-year-old daughter landed five As and two A stars in her GCSE exams (entrance exams for the next higher school) and I never once said to her she *had to* do it. I just said, "Well, you can't do any worse than I did." My fifteen-year-old son landed at least nine As and a scholarship at school. But then my wife and I always have had a more liberal approach. I have never pushed them to pass anything—quite the opposite, actually.

Intelligence works the other way too: seeing what you *don't* need to learn. Why would I need to memorize the periodic table of elements? I didn't care if I couldn't climb a rope in the school gym, dissect a garden frog, or play the recorder. And what was the point of long division or memorizing Latin verbs and the Greek names of cells that we find in a common weed?

That's why we invented the word "failure" in the first place, to try to put people who are wildly creative in a place. All kids who don't pass are failures, and that's not right.

Today I speak at schools all over the world, and I love all the teachers I meet. It's a tough job teaching from a set-in-concrete curriculum. How curious is it that the biggest failure on the planet, with straight fails in all his exams, is speaking at schools and universities across the globe and writing books? There's more than one path to success. We all go our own ways. No one should *ever* be called a failure by the system, or by anyone else for that matter as there's no such thing.

CHAPTER 7

Finishing School

After the school clamped down on me bringing products in, I was reduced to a new smuggling operation and began trading more secretly in the corner of the playground or the back of morning assembly. I managed to continue swapping sweets for pens, calculators, and even watches and got away with this for the first couple terms, but it all came to an abrupt end when my trading was eventually discovered. I had swapped my last supplies of popping candy for a rather expensive Parker pen with a boy from one of the wealthier families. I had never had such a fine instrument to write with! It had a particularly shiny gold nib. I used to look at the letters etched on the nib, "18 ct gold," which made me feel so rich! My cheap and nasty fountain pens leaked continuously, and both my index finger and the outside of my blazer pockets were permanently stained blue from them.

It was a genuine trade-off—my friend was delighted to have some popping candy in return for his classy pen, and I was happy that my fingers were finally going back to their original color. His parents, however, were understandably not so keen on the deal. They wrote to the school, and subsequently I had to return it along with many other traded items. My swaps had come to an end. However, I had learned valuable new skills, namely meeting people and trading. Eventually these made me a lot of money. Paradoxically, I was learning a lot of essential life skills in school after all.

A lot of the kids would tell me about their new products and what they tasted like and why they liked them, so I stumbled into writing. I finally asked my mum if she wanted me to pen something for the magazine about the sweets, in particular what the kids thought of the candy I was giving out. If you think about it, that's exactly what confectionery producers like to know.

Because she was short of writers who would write for free and unable to pay her staff, my mum gradually ushered me in to learn how to edit and write about the products. It was a clever idea, as even though my writing skills were questionable, she spotted my flare for it and the readers moreover were able to get a snapshot inside school life.

Little did I know that some confectionery giants would read my words. Admittedly at the beginning it was a pretty bad standard, heavily edited, and not much went into print; it started as more of a cartoon with a caption. But by the time I was fifteen, I managed to produce a small, profoundly amended column called Sweetspot. My job was to edit down all the press releases from around the world, the latest news on new products and factory equipment, and the terrible photos of new marketing managers that I couldn't believe anyone would actually be interested in. I was cynical, and it worked in my favor, as journalists are taught to question everything. At last I was pleased to be able to say I was doing something constructive.

In the meantime, it was the popping candy that kept me going. The kids went wild over the stuff, asking all the time for more as it was not for sale yet in the United Kingdom. I continued where I could to trade with it. Shortly after, it was launched in the UK and it became a huge craze around the world. They are still in circulation in the confectionery market today, now known as Pop Rocks.

The months passed and finally came the summer of 1975, and I snapped up my three-month trip to America. I was to stay in a most welcoming place that I had never heard of called Vermont and spend the summer with a distant godmother and family who knew of our troubles and decided to help. I also discovered that I had a distant aunt in Boston, who was living there with my grandmother on my father's side who had recently moved there, and I got to see her.

My American experience and road trip were a complete surprise to us all. I loved everything about the United States—the superior sporting facilities (they actually had running tracks), the warm weather, the huge size of everything, the open and welcoming people, and the spectacular scenery of the Connecticut River. I found the whole country impossible to believe, especially after they announced that we were going to drive to Wyoming from Vermont on a massive tour in an old Volvo and back through Canada, past the Great Lakes.

I think when you live in an area like I do in Southeast England, one of the most overcrowded parts of Europe, you can only dream of open roads and miles and miles of countryside where you never meet anyone. With sixty-six million people in our tiny country and most of them in the Southeast, overcrowding is a constant problem. I can't get a doctor's appointment for three weeks, as they are too busy to see me. Everything everywhere is full, from schools to waiting lists for surgery to tables for dinner. There is no space to live and hardly a park to walk in; you find yourself with thousands of others with the same idea wherever you go.

In the States, it just all seemed easier. You could get up and go, at least once you'd left the big cities. I know the US has massive traffic problems in some areas, too, but it seems, at least from the experiences I had, that once you leave the big cities there is just so much space to escape to. Here you never really escape.

I remember sleeping out in a Wyoming national park with a sleeping bag and a log fire and looking for my connection with the stars in the sky before I slept. I'll never forget that. I also learned to ride a horse, which I love. Sadly, over here in the UK, it seems like a rich person's hobby. The land is too expensive.

I fit easily into the way of life in the US. My mentor in the country, the father of the boy with whom I was staying, was a well-known hematologist. I learned a lot from him and his wife, and they really helped with my healing process following the bereavement. Being a doctor, he was well trained in counseling patients and relatives close to death, so I had weeks of counseling without knowing it.

For once in my life I had two parents (okay, not mine) who wanted to listen to me and my story. I realized that I had never spoken to anyone about my mother's booze cruises and the loss. He was a lovely man, and his wife was the perfect person for me at the time, always taking care of me and giving me her time and attention. My trip to America was a giant healing process in every way. I've lost touch with the family now. One day I hope to find them in Vermont and thank them. I don't think they realized the monumental effect their plan had on me. Without them, I could easily have gone the other way.

Unsurprisingly, I really didn't want to return to the depression of failing school tests, smoky buses, inedible school blancmange-pudding lunches, and a houseful of empty gin bottles. After the most spectacular summer of my life in the US, I had to board the Pan Am flight home and prepare to sit for an exam called the 11 Plus.

Shortly after my return from the United States, my mother came back from the school parents' evening saying that I wasn't going to sit for the exams at all, as it was decided I wasn't ready for them. I am not sure if it was her demand; knowing her, I am sure she put her foot down. She wasn't the sort of person people would argue with. She almost drowned the swimming teacher when she heard he used to throw kids who couldn't swim in the deep end of the pool, thinking it might make them swim. He was a cruel man and the kids were totally terrified, shaking with fear as they lined up to plunge in. I watched her almost two hundred pounds come in handy as she smothered him underwater like a subarctic walrus protecting its young. She had a great sense of justice. So no one in the school argued with her, I wasn't sitting for the exams and she became the school hero.

Nonetheless, I had to study hard for the following sufficiently overhyped exam, this one called the Common Entrance Examination. It's the big one, apparently, that gets you into the top schools at thirteen years old. As far as I could see, my entrance would be mostly uncommon, and that's all there was to it.

Well, it wasn't much of a surprise to anyone that after another two years of very little studying, I didn't manage to score high enough to get into a top-grade good school. I eventually took the exams two years later and failed every subject. And then the day came for *me* to put my foot down. I finally told my mother to forget it all and not to worry about my education, and that she was wasting her time on me. She was really beginning to wonder what she should do with me. Equally, I had no idea what I was to do with her, so we made a great pair worrying about each other.

I explained that I couldn't see the point of going to school, but she persisted for two years, coming up with various new and ever-desperate educational plans, but it was mainly her listening to promises from headmasters announcing they would make me into a super exam star. In the end, I went to thirteen schools before my mother finally gave up.

I learned a lot through the failures. Because I went to so many places, I furthered my ability to meet people—another extremely useful skill. After I failed my exams, I agreed to have one last try in the local free school.

It was scary at first, being the new boy at school, but I had become perfectly accustomed to being placed in new situations and almost forced to go up to people I had never met. As I had attended so many schools, it was now normal to be abnormal.

Life settled down into a manageable rhythm of failure. My mother had her full attention on the bottle while I paid the *least* attention to my schoolbooks: both of us feeling triumphant in the process.

I eventually learned to get my head down, accept the system in which I found myself, and get on with it, but this particular free school wasn't so friendly. This was to be my final school.

My name was written on the bathroom wall in a black marker pen with those of a few other sad kids, which meant I was going to get a school welcome: a kicking from the resident thug. Apparently there was no escape from this prehistoric pastime.

As opposed to meeting and getting to know people, this school seemed to be all about fighting new arrivals and doing its best to make them feel miserable. It certainly had a bad reputation as being one of the worst in the area. The school bully was in the grade above me, and his job was to make sure that any "threats," such as popular kids with endless supplies of bubble gum and chews that mopped up attention, were weeded out at a suitably early stage.

My elder brother by two years, James, was at boarding school, and by now he was into powerlifting and weight training. He honestly looked like the Hulk. I phoned him and told him about the problem.

"Do the unexpected," he advised. "Give him some candy before the fight, or if that doesn't work, if he's bigger than you, try winding him. That means getting him from behind and squeezing his stomach fast and rapidly. It winds them, and he will expect you to try and punch him, so he won't expect that. Bribe him with chocolate first."

I practiced my bear hugs at home on my poor defenseless pillows for the next few days. In the end, I became well rehearsed at it, bursting several pillows in front of my confused canine audience. I thought about the offering of sweets, but I never got the opportunity and wondered whether it was just a form of giving in.

My big day came, much to the frenzied delight of the other kids, who created a giant circle crowding round and forming an unofficial ring. My opponent was waiting in the middle, allowing the attention to fuel his ego. I was pushed through to meet my competitor, who drew on his cigarette and gave himself the time to sum me up. I reached into my pockets but just had an old packet of Opal Fruit chews, hardly an ego match for his big boy cigarettes, so I left the sweets in my pocket and resigned myself to the ridiculous task ahead.

I stood there watching him, wondering what I should do. A last-minute offering, perhaps? I couldn't just allow this person to hit me, but I had resigned myself to the fact that I had better get on with it and satisfy this tribal approach to school life. He started to move closer and fired a huge kick at me, which I tried to punch out of the way—a really stupid thing to do, as I felt a crack in my hand as my fingers made contact with his steel-toed boots.

That wasn't what I had planned. I ran to the side. But several kids pushed me back and egged me on while I thought hard about my next move and tried to ignore the increasing pain in my hand. No time for that. He started to come at me again, looking pleased at the pain he caused and wanting more. I ran at him, trying to rugby tackle him, and to be honest it wasn't at all heroic. It was messy, and I must have looked very ill prepared. Fighting was definitely a new thing for me. He kicked me again and caught me in the thigh, and it really did hurt this time. I didn't like that. There was another cheer of satisfaction from the crowd feeding off my radiating pain, each of them betting I would now go down first.

I had to do *something*. I was not going to be beaten that easily, and besides, how dare he just kick me and laugh. Now I was really close to him, dodging punches and blows that were coming one after the other. I had to position myself behind him. His punches were thundering down on me. *Blimey, he's good at this*, I thought, *he must do it all the time*. I remembered what my brother said as the blows came pounding in over my head and back as I crouched down. *If I don't get to hug him I'm finished*, I thought. The crowd by now was ecstatic, wanting to see more pain at every moment and hopefully some blood for good effect.

I noticed he was breathing heavily. His smoking certainly wasn't helping him. I somehow managed to get behind him and then, just like in my practice on the pillow, I yanked my fists into the soft part of his stomach and squeezed him as hard I could muster.

This unexpected movement took him by surprise; my fists sunk deep into his stomach. It was very soft and there was no resistance. I must have really squashed his organs. He dropped to his knees in fits of coughing, cursing, and spitting at the crowd. He looked like he was going to throw up. I had no idea how effective this would be, but it certainly seemed to have the desired effect. His lungs weren't in a good condition anyway, so unwittingly I seemed to have hit his weakest point. The crowd roared up again and now his supporters seemed to turn on him, egging me on to kick the bully and finally see their feast of blood.

I wasn't in a brilliant state myself. I stood over him and could have kicked him, but I'm glad I didn't. I was especially happy the whole episode had been brought to a welcome end. My assailant decided that it was enough too. Not wanting people to see him winded, he pushed a group of cheering kids out of his way and marched off to the toilet, the place where he might have realized he'd made a mistake in writing my name on the wall.

I wasn't sure what to do after that. I hadn't won or lost in my opinion, so I followed him. I made my way out of the commotion, confused as to why we both frantically hit each other without knowing each other and then tried to walk away from it all. I followed him into the boys' changing rooms and sat next to him. Now was the time to offer him my chews. He was astonished at my offering as I peeled back the wrapper.

No one was supposed to *like* him. It seemed that the candies hit harder than any blow he had ever received. That day, we became good friends, though it seems a plainly ridiculous way to get to know someone: hit each other randomly for no set time and then eat Opal Fruit chews together.

Sadly, we did not stay friends for long, but for a few days I got to know him well. He confided in me before I left the school. Like me, he had endured a rough time at home through a broken family. We had a lot in common in some ways.

After the fight, the results of which were a broken little finger and a few bruises, my mother decided I wasn't in the best academic environment and came up with yet another new idea, which actually was the best yet. I was to homeschool from then on. She finally gave in. My days at school were officially over. She had given up talking to teachers about me, so it was a welcome relief for a young teenager who had just about lost faith in all subjects taught and life in general.

I never lost faith in the teachers, as they were always really friendly and doing their jobs. I was pleased that they didn't have to put up with me after that and thanked them for persisting nevertheless. On a tearful last day, I took in carrier bags full of boxes of chocolates to give to them all and apologized for being so useless at my work. It was one of the most powerful things I ever did, to apologize with a lovely gift for being such a blatant school disaster. There were a lot of tears on that day, from me, too, but mainly from relief that the farcical tests would soon be over.

Homeschooling it was to be. My school days were now done and dusted and I officially left school with nothing at fourteen years old. My next school was the infamous House of Candy and Cocktails at Muswell Hill. During the day, I would pretend to be doing my home-school work when my mother was awake and I would skateboard in the garden on a new ramp I built for myself while she slept.

But then something happened quite naturally. While she slept, I found myself answering the office phone. Over time, I got to know people and customers, and I must say I learned quickly to master the telephone. I enjoyed chatting with the people who, for obvious reasons, could never seem to get through to my mother. Many of them I had met in Germany, so we already knew each other and just got to chatting.

I would converse for hours with customers, and they seemed to like my original about-to-break voice. I would come up with new and elaborate reasons for my mother's continuous absence, saying she was in meetings with important people or talking to banks, major confectioners, and suppliers; the truth was that she was behind me snoring over the IBM typewriter.

They loved it, and soon I was learning how to influence people and get them on my side over the phone. This is an excellent skill for selling advertising—actually, an excellent skill for selling anything. It was something I became so good at that I would go on to sell millions and millions of dollars' worth of advertising for the magazine. I was indirectly selling, and I was also writing professionally at sixteen years old without an English qualification. I can still sell anything to anyone. It's not really about making someone do something; it's just a natural thing to help someone find a nice solution and home for their hard-earned money.

I continued to write. I read the news that came in about the industry every day and learned quickly about the world of chocolate and candy.

Unfortunately, my homeschooling books were never opened, especially when there were sweets in the mail for me and the dogs to take care of first. And it soon became clear to everyone that even with the homeschooling, I wasn't going to pass anything. And even though both my parents went to Trinity College in Dublin and my grandfather was in the MI6 intelligence service, Angus Kennedy wasn't going to fly that flag and follow their suit. I was going to be the first in line to mess it all up. However, my grandfather was on the booze and my mother joined him; I managed to stop that particular line of disaster, which seemed to get handed down over the generations. I picked the right thing in which to succeed.

My brother, amazingly, managed to get at least thirteen passes in his GCSE exams and won a scholarship to one of the top public schools in the country, while my sister was long gone reading history at university. And there I was, the candy kid with no apparent future.

Not that I ever worried about it. After my start in life, nothing mattered, so I let everyone else do the worrying about my life instead. At times, I had tried hard at some subjects I liked, like art and geography, but I still never managed to get better than a straight fail or a U, which means it was so bad it was unclassified.

My previous English teacher had lost hope for me at school. My writing was highly creative with wild ideas and I already had a different agenda for learning. I couldn't help it. I would even write graphic descriptions of my teachers and how I perceived them while they were teaching us in class and duly hand them my work. It wasn't derogatory in any way, but it *was* the truth, and not all the teachers were that savory, to say the least. Everything was described, from their mannerisms to the well-rehearsed, meaningless overused sayings that one or two would repeat constantly. I would describe it all and greatly compliment some of my teachers, too. I am sure the staff might have blamed my poor English teacher for creating such a sharp-eyed critical monster.

Writing for me was about reaction. None of my work ever received good grades, but I still churned out the stories with great imagination and detail, even though the grammar was dreadful. Writing poetry and stories seemed to be the only constant in my life. I have thousands of poems, some I have never bothered to read again. I never showed them to the teachers, my mother, no one. Perhaps I should have.

But to the understandable frustration of my teachers, I never worried about things like punctuation, as its focus interfered with the flow of creative energy. If you focus on the worry about something, it stumps the flow. English comprehension, I detested greatly. In my opinion, if we didn't understand a text, then it was by a rubbish writer. It was plainly the writer's fault if they did not make it clear or engage the reader. How the teachers managed to consistently find *the* most boring pieces to study was quite an achievement in itself.

But my English teacher was right: I would never pass an exam without the correct grammar. She was paid to teach me that grammar, but I was born to write. I am glad I have stuck at what I was born to do. So many gifts are distinguished at school. It seems to me that you can pen the most spectacularly boring piece (a party political broadcast for example) and still get an A-plus as long as it was technically correct. The system hardly encouraged creativity back then, I hope it has changed. But the system failed me; I never failed the system, none of us did. The whole government education system is a spectacular failure if you see it for what it really is.

While going through the attic, I recently found an old schoolbook that contained one of my stories. It was a good story (I loved it) but I was marked down to 2 out of 20 with a note: "Angus, why don't you ever, ever read through and check your work?" I was surprised to find my own reply written underneath the teacher's comment: "Because you have just checked it for me."

So when the day came for my homeschool GCSE level exams, I was brilliantly prepared to fail them all. I studied at home, so that meant taking my exams in hotels and town halls. I took biology five times and failed every time. I just could not see the point in remembering the properties of xylem and phloem. Did I really need to know about random parts of plants when most people that come out of school don't even know how to pay a utility bill or open a bank account?

The gentleman at the door of the exam hall started to recognize me, as I kept going back every few months for another retake of my biology test. He taught me more than the whole course. The last time I went along for my final attempt, I arrived at the exam door and noted that he was still working there.

"You're back," he said. "Man, you don't give up, do you? Just wait till it's something you *really want to do*, and then nothing on earth will stop you; nothing, son. That's what I like to see. Someone who never gives up."

He was right, of course, because if you don't give up, you are a success. We may keep failing, but it's only because no one has shown us anything at which we can be successful.

So now having failed all my GCSE exams so spectacularly, I had to cheat to get into college. When the results came through the post showing so many fails, I whited out a few exam certificates and changed one of the Us to a passing C grade. I always knew my artistic skill would come in handy one day.

It was a cheap trick that I am not overly proud of, I admit, but I managed to land a place at one of the best art colleges in the country on the strength of my portfolio. The college seemed to like radicals, and they found my drawings and novel ideas so unusual that I wangled a place with ease. Eventually from there I went on to get a place at university to study photographic journalism. But still I hadn't actually passed anything to date. Yes, a complete fraud and fake, perhaps. I finally entered the gates of the dizzy heights of which I didn't really deserve but I was there, and after the first year, the course was even going well. I wondered if finally, after years and years, I was going to get an academic qualification after all. Would I, like my brother and sister, be able to invite my mum to my graduation? Would I, too, be good enough for the black-and-white photo on the mantelpiece with my mum on my graduation day with a mortarboard on my head? What would they be proud of with Angus? I really struggled to find anything I had actually achieved and remember telling my mum those very words. I was a spectacular failure already.

However, I was about to be the closest I have *ever* been to both dying and passing a test. The only thing I passed this time, though, was out. It took years to recover, and the police thought it was attempted murder. My education was about to receive its final blow.

CHAPTER 8

Murder?

I was now nineteen years old and I was at the stage of my finals, a critical time for my university degree. It was late at night and I was on my way to Camden Town to watch a band playing, when I was hit hard with what must have been a baseball bat.

The bat caught me around the jaw and to the side of my head. The horrible crack to my temple reverberated through my body. I was knocked out clean and collapsed into a small alley, lying face down in the gutter. I felt myself being dragged across the pavement to a quieter spot where I wouldn't be seen.

The odd thing was that I was conscious of my attackers. So even though I couldn't see them, I could tell that there must only have been two or three of them at most. One dragged me over and the others, I could feel, went through my inside jacket pocket and trousers while I was lying on the ground. They just wanted my money, I guess. I could hear their ugly voices but couldn't see them or twist my neck around or open my eyes. I was at the mercy of my assailants, my face pressed in the side of the road, just able to breathe with my lips open to the grit.

I saw strange bright lights spinning all over my body. The bright lights were coming to take me away, and what a welcome experience it was to be so distant—it was really appealing. It then went totally black, the lights vanished, and that was it. I was in a void between heaven and Earth, a place most of us are not allowed to remember, including me, and how frustrating that was.

My body could have been anywhere—the gutter, anywhere, who knows? I couldn't have *that* many lives, come on! Not even chocolate could save me this time.

But time passed. A few hours, a day, a night? I had no idea. I eventually came around. I could hear distant traffic, but I couldn't see anything. I managed to get myself up to my feet but found it difficult to stay upright without keeling over. I reached for my eyes and stroked my cheeks. There was swelling and dried blood around my eyes, so no wonder I couldn't see. I didn't think it was night, but I couldn't be sure.

I stumbled around what I imagined to be a sidewalk by scraping my feet along the cracks. What a sight I must have been. I heard the occasional car or truck pass. Was I on the road? What if I was? Surely I would be polished off and run over. With one of my arms stretched out in front of me feeling my way, I called out for help.

My voice wasn't working and I couldn't open my mouth. My jaw would not budge. Oh dear, what had I done now?

And where was everyone? No one came to help. I was sure I could hear the sound of footsteps, of people walking right past me. I felt faint and was going to fall. Would I get up at all next time? My breath was out of control, and I could feel an inescapable panic coming on. *I'm blind, can't stand, there's a lot of blood, it's really not so good*, I thought. *Someone help me. Angus, surely now you're knocking on the door for another life?*

The physical pain was bad enough, but no one coming to help hurt more than the first blow. Perhaps people thought they might get hit too, if they helped me. Whatever the reason, I needed medical attention, as at any minute my lights would go out.

I had no idea if I was on the road or the sidewalk as I took each step forward. I remember thinking, *You had better do something quick, or you are going back to the stars (no matter how tempting that may be!).* I put my hand up to my head again. It was cold, sticky, and all sorts of debris was stuck to my face. I must have been lying outside for some time after being dragged off somewhere so the crime would be hidden. Perhaps my assailants thought I was dead. I must have been quite an unpleasant sight.

I couldn't feel my face. The nerves started to shut down as I lost sensation in my lips, cheeks, and bottom-left eyelid. I couldn't feel anything, and things were shutting down fast. It was as if I was touching someone else's face, not mine. The body's way of taking the pain away?

I pulled my eyelid up to create a gap, but I couldn't really see much. I must have looked like a man right out of a horror movie. People probably thought I was playing a joke on my way to a prize-giving zombie party. I noticed the smell of coffee as I shuffled forward and knew that it was no longer nighttime. I had been out cold for most of the night and woken up in the early morning.

What do you do when you feel you have hours left, your body fueled on adrenaline only, you are in the center of a city (you think), and no one is helping you?

I had to fake an accident on the road. My legs were shaking, feelings and nerves were shutting down, and not only was I blind with smashed bones all over my face, but I now also felt a new sense of confusion and panic, a far more formidable opponent.

However, a kind of gentle fog was seeping into my mind to take the horror away, the sort of fog that lets you fall gracefully and drift away with a smile on your face.

It was a dangerous move to lie on the road, but even though I was on the way out, I really did think clearly. Besides, if I waited for another idea it might be one idea too late. No choice. You don't *think* how to survive in a situation like that, you function on instinct. If I faked being hit by a car, perhaps people would see it was safe to help me. I was a real person in understandable trouble. I wasn't a drug user or a prize medical specimen that had escaped from the zombie lab. I listened to the cars, worked out roughly where the road was, and made my way over.

I felt the curb with my hands and walked a few paces onto the road.

What a stupid thing to do! a voice in my head screamed.

I dropped to my knees and ran my fingers across the smooth tarmac surface of the road. Then I crawled a few final paces and collapsed onto the main road, on my side. I could hear the cars going by. This was it, then. I braced myself. It was time to say goodbye to the taste of chocolate and life; amen. I could not see if a car was coming or not.

A few terrible moments passed as I drifted off and prepared myself to wake up on my distant star. Maybe it was my time. I was on the verge of death again, but this time it was someone's choice to take away my life, no nasty bacteria, flames, or bad food. If I had no medical attention this time, I knew I didn't have long, or perhaps I would just be squashed by a delivery van.

Was it worse to be murdered by the villains that hit me, or be ignored by normal people and left to suffer? Was I committing suicide by lying in the road? And then what of my poor mum? She would think I had ended my life when I hadn't done anything of the sort.

I drifted off again and then was woken by the majestic sound of a woman's voice.

"My God, he's been hit by a car. How could they drive off? Someone call an ambulance, he's still breathing. Call an ambulance, quick," she screamed. A powerful cocktail of hearing and hope was just about all I had left to go on.

I felt her pull a coat over me, and I started to cry with relief. A mixture of tears and blood painted a tapestry of pain down my face. This was *my* angel and she was perfectly human, too. I loved this woman. If only I could have seen her and thanked her.

"Are you okay? What's your name?"

I couldn't talk.

"What happened to you?"

When people think they understand what has happened, they help. Instinct probably told previous passersby that they were in danger if they came to the aid of a man wandering around the street looking like a squashed scarlet shield bug. I will never know. But I do remember the musical sounds of more people rushing in to help me. Many more pedestrians now gathered around me. One voice turned into three, six, a dozen. Finally, a policeman arrived—another angel.

Soon I was hyperventilating with the delayed shock and dipping in and out of consciousness. The hyperventilation was making me take in too much oxygen, so the policeman got a paper bag to help me breathe, helping me inhale my own expelled air, reducing the intake of oxygen. Above all, he spoke to me and kept me going. I wish I could find him and that amazing woman and thank them both, but I never saw them again. The policeman would say he was just doing his job, but I would say he was doing far more than that.

I ended up on a trolley in the hospital's Accident & Emergency ward with a broken skull and a jaw in all sorts of unrequested angles. My eye had dropped a few millimeters, and my head had swollen to the size of a large watermelon. It took a few days for one eye to open itself and another twenty years for the feeling to return to my lips and face. I couldn't have a too-hot cup of tea for years after without realizing I was burning my face.

When my mother did eventually arrive through the swinging doors of the hospital corridor, she walked straight past my trolley. Whether that was the drink or the fact I bore no resemblance to her son was another matter.

I stayed in the hospital for weeks and was unable to eat properly for months, as my jaw was so badly damaged and wired up. It was soft foods and guess what else for weeks on end?

Chocolate.

Again.

I can't say chocolate *saved* my life, but it was all I really wanted to eat and all I could eat, and anyway there was a good supply. It kind of cheered me up to have it piled next to the hospital bed and it made me super popular with the nurses and patients. So once again I had to thank the confections—and of course my heroes and doctors—for bringing me back to life.

The lengthy hospital stay sealed my fate. I was really going to have no academic passes whatsoever. I couldn't honestly continue with my degree in journalism after missing so much coursework. Even though University of Nottingham was very accommodating, it was clear that I had lost interest after the drama, so that spelled the end of my formal education for good. That will teach me for cheating, hey?

Following the attack, the police wanted to catch my assailants and convict them of attempted murder. I had several interviews with the police detectives at the side of my hospital bed, but no one was ever caught. So now I guess I can lay claim to the fact that I have survived a murder attempt, too. There was a series of operations afterward to raise my eye, push my zygomatic bone out to its original position, and make good the troublesome angles that lay claim to my face; they literally rebuilt my head. (To recover, I had more chocolate.)

I also managed to claim on our insurance quite a sizable sum of money in those days of a few thousand pounds. So I came out of university with no qualifications at all but also no debt. On the contrary, I was one of the only people to have a large sum of cash instead of a degree. Quite a result!

After my attack, I got the message: I wasn't going to get any qualifications or pass *anything* for that matter, and it was time to close the chapters once and for all.

It's important not to accept defeat—and my motto is "never give up"—but I do believe in listening to the inner voice that calmly says enough is enough. There had to be another way to succeed. It was time for me to leave, not only the education system but the country completely.

CHAPTER 9

Working in a Mint Factory

I came out of university early, at the age of twenty, and gradually recovered from the murder attempt, but my mother's health deteriorated rapidly. Over the next twenty grueling years, the alcohol would start to destroy her liver, brain, and most of her body in earnest. She began putting on weight fast and retaining water. Every cell in her body seemed to swell up. I won't go into too many details, as this is, after all, a book about chocolate and not about a decaying mother!

Once upon a time she used to be able to walk, she used to eat, and we would go for long walks in London's parks during her rare sober moments. But over the years I noticed that normal day-to-day things she did like wash, sleep, take time out, clean up, brush her hair, converse, and really just live normally all seemed to stop, one after the other. She was like an office block shutting down in the evening, gradually all her lights were going out.

It's a very subtle process. You never actually see your kids grow up, you just see one day that they are taller than you or can swim faster. Likewise it dawned on me that my mother was a vegetable. She had stopped eating properly and only put stuff on the plate to make me think she was going to eat. Other things were easy to spot, like not washing or taking even the slightest concern in the way she looked. But that was nothing. I could take her alarming looks and see my mother turn into a rotting vegetable every day, but smelling like one was another ball game altogether.

I'm not joking when I say that she could clear a pub bar in minutes when I wheeled her in her wheelchair. Even without her in the chair, which was a rare occasion, as she slept in it too, you could smell the chair on its own from a distance. Not long before she died, when I was forty-one, the smell was so bad that it could make you physically sick if you were not used to it. Can you imagine a woman who never washes? People certainly get out of the way. I would spray her with perfumes and anything I could get my hands on before she went out.

Imagine your girlfriend asking to see your mother and getting upset because you are reticent. No one can really understand. The pungent smell was sickly sweet, it was beyond recognizable and one you will never forget.

I was amazed each day she woke up. It came to the stage that the ambulance men refused to come out to "the drunk." It takes a very strong person to pick someone up off the floor and clear the mess. Somehow I did it and when my brother was around he did too. I stayed with her until the final day, and this is where much of my strength comes from today.

She was very heavy toward the end—she must have been more than two hundred pounds—and I had to pick her up a few times. I stuck at it and stood up for her until the day she finally passed away. It was a day of gigantic relief for both my mother and me, the whole family too, relieved the pain was all finally over.

You don't get any certificates or grades for taking care of people, and to cap it all—can you believe it?—people blamed my family and me for not looking after her. We even had customers of the magazine who decided not to advertise with us, saying we didn't help her. You can't win with an alcoholic. Loving a victim like my mother was a difficult thing to do, but it sculpts you into a great person, if you come out on top. I know a lot of kids with parents on the way to alcoholism, and I try hard to help them understand that they are not at fault, they are doing all they can. We can only learn to accept.

———————

After I returned from failing my exams at university, a good twenty years before my mother got into the late stages of alcohol abuse, a true miracle happened. Out of the blue, my mother met an ex–German soldier named Walter. He was another angel. He was a survivor who had been shot through the neck on the Russian front. You could see the scars on his neck where the bullet had entered and exited. He went through far worse than I could ever imagine, especially being ordered to do terrible things by the SS. In comparison my mum was a piece of cake.

He seemed to pop out of heaven. She met him at a press conference as he also worked in the publishing trade. He took it all on, and helped me put things into perspective again. The new duo got on with the job. Walter helped with the business and helped my mother even more, and they made each other very happy. While he was with her, at last, my opportunity came to live *my* life.

I couldn't stay at home. My education had been a spectacular failure, so the time had come to leave the house for a few months, away from all the illness and bad luck. I felt I could cope with just about anything life could throw at me. With nothing to lose, I didn't really care anymore about succeeding or failing.

The world was open to me, and it was time to go and make it even sweeter. All I knew was candy, and I had a few contacts that I had written about for the magazine. So, naturally, I went to work in a candy factory.

I chose to work in Germany after getting to know Walter, who spoke a lot about Germany and the German people. I wondered if his experiences there led to his refreshing and spontaneous attitude toward life. Even though I loved Muswell Hill, I hadn't really experienced that much life overseas apart from a few campsites in the Isle of Wight and my US tour.

I decided to make mints in the Black Forest. One of the people I got to know through the magazine invited me out to his factory near Karlsruhe in Southern Germany to work. How perfect was this? I was ready in a few days, and off I went to the peppermint plant for several months, to work every day making super-hot breath-freshening mints.

In medieval Europe, people used to mix mint plants with vinegar to make a mouthwash to freshen breath. In 1790, during the reign of King George III, mint lozenges called Altoids were invented by a London-based company called Smith & Company to freshen breath. Eventually, production stopped in Wales and continued in the United States.

Later, commercially made hard mints using peppermint oils were sold in Victorian England. Rudeness was practically an executable offense in the Victorian era, so fresh breath was essential. These mints were made from boiled sugar, cut using a rotary tablet press, and distributed throughout Europe and the United States.

But I didn't learn a huge amount about the history of mints as I had hoped, or anything else at my new job. I was stationed in the packaging department. I thought I would be helping create new mint wonders for the market and stirring giant pots. No such luck. The big factories are all about machines. I was assigned to a machine, *my* machine, which I naively found almost exciting at first. But that didn't last long, say an hour or two.

My machine kept breaking down, so they needed a real human— that is, me—to attend to this ailing piece of 1960s equipment and correct its regular fault every few minutes.

My job was to give the tubes of sweets a helpful little shove on the conveyor belt each minute, to help them on their journey into the wrapping machine. It was mind-blowingly boring. After my first few days, I could have stared at a plain white recycled toilet-paper roll from the supermarket for three hours and found it acutely interesting. The dream of working in a weird and wonderful candy factory is not what we all imagine. Well, not my job anyway.

Every day, every hour, shift by shift, week by week, I dreamed of the tea breaks to rescue my sanity. It was the closest I have ever been to actually becoming a machine. Of course, the entire experience was not helped at all by my inability to converse with anyone, as they all spoke German.

Modern factories (the larger ones, anyway) are now increasingly all about artificially intelligent machines and clever ingredients. Most of the big ones are very high tech, fully equipped with these artificially intelligent systems that tell you if a part needs replacing or if they aren't running as efficiently as they could be running, reminding their owners to look after them properly.

A modern chocolate factory is absolutely nothing like what you see in *Charlie and the Chocolate Factory*, which incidentally breaks just about every health and safety regulation on the planet.

I was not to be defeated by boredom, so I set myself a challenge to see how long I could stick to what was one of the most boring jobs in Europe. Even if it was mind-numbing, it was a job, and my first job, too. I soon discovered that a string of similar failed students and dropouts like me had been assigned this job, the worst in the factory. The other workers seemed to be doing interesting things, like moving from one machine to another, sweeping floors, and walking through strange, see-through plastic swing doors, which meant they were able to see what was on the other side in the other room, beyond my permitted territory.

It was a low-paying job, too. I had to be up at 5:00 a.m., and I was a temporary guest worker. I guess the other workers knew there was no real point getting to know the next candy-into-the-wrapping-machine shover. How long would this one last?

But my resilience was helped greatly by the fact that I met a very attractive German girl and spent a lot of time with her in the evenings after work. Things were looking good, and soon, not only was I the fastest stick-wrapping-machine operator, but I was also quickly becoming fluent in my first foreign language. This was due to the fact that I loved listening to anything my new girlfriend said, even though I didn't understand a word at first. As a result, all these years later, more than half of my clients are from Germany. Germany has a very strong confectionery manufacturing industry, and along with the Swiss, Dutch, and Italians, they make some of the best confectionery processing and packing machines in the world.

Once I had mastered my newfound skill of assisting a machine, the boredom forced me to try new and more adventurous things. I built a couch shape out of the mint packets that spewed out the other side of my failing piece of equipment, providing a resting place for workers to relax.

When it was complete, I stood back and marveled at my new sculpture. Completing it took several hours, which of course I had available, as I gave up trying to rescue my machine and let the mints get stuck deliberately, thus making the whole thing break down.

Sweet.

This provided me with lots of time to get on with the more important task of being an artist. I carefully laid each packet out and built my couch, much to the delight of other workers, who knew my fate was rushing toward me at lightning speed.

I sat on my homemade couch and rested the aching discs in my back at the very moment my manager walked in. To my surprise, his initial reaction was one of genuine amusement, and I eventually got away with a warning that my candy sculpture department had breached health and safety regulations. However, the following week the boredom hit me again. This time I made an armchair, which was even better. I got quite a name for myself.

Finally, and I guess rightly, my manager had seen enough. My approach was not assisting the speed of the production of mints, and I was sent on my way.

I tried not to think about it, but I had been fired for the first time in my life from the only proper job I had ever held. I really had nothing going for me, no money, no qualifications, and only a bit of German. I could make a couch out of peppermints, something for my CV, but that was it.

In reality, with a dwindling bank balance, no qualifications to get me a higher-paying job, and no skills to do anything, plus my mother's business and health not going well, things looked a little bleak again. Man plans and then God laughs.

One thing I always did was dream of the successful years to come. I knew in my heart that it would all be better one day. Still, hope is good for breakfast but not for tea; you can't survive on hope and wishes all the time. But you can still keep believing in yourself. I always believed, and still do, that it's going to get better all the time, because what else *can* we do? That's faith.

I returned to the UK with my outstandingly useless skills and the door open for me to enter the dwindling publishing business run by a complete alcoholic. No one else would take me. However I was now bilingual, which happened to be extremely useful and a huge surprise to my German stepfather. It pleased him greatly before his death, which was soon after my return.

I had no idea how talented I was. I knew how to meet people from going to so many schools. I was fearless as I had lost so much, and I could trade and sell as I used to swap and sell sweets. Life had taught me the most important skills in business.

Trade publishing is quite boring. Of course, as you can imagine, chocolate is a great industry and subject in which to find oneself, though you don't want to be writing about vertical form fill seal-packaging technology or extrusion equipment for your whole life, no matter how much money it earns. You have to keep looking to the big picture.

Sadly, following my stepfather's passing, my mother became more ill, and so whether I liked it or not, I had to attend to the helm of a failing publishing business with my brother, who had returned from university. The company was in the red with no funds, little advertising, and few readers, and to be honest it was not something I or he, I believe, really wanted to work for. However, with my abilities to meet people, trade, sell anything to anyone, and chat on the phone with ease, plus being bilingual, I was well positioned to get into anything. But I had no idea what loomed within and it was inadvertently that I had acquired the key skills for making money.

With a creative, no-fear attitude toward losing everything, I soon confirmed that I could sell just about anything. My brother ran the accounts and administration, and we eventually took it from a loss leader to a very profitable company, which made my mother very happy.

It was a satisfying ending to my mother's great career in publishing. She finished on a good note. It wasn't long after she saw that the business was going well that she passed away. She died in publishing, and that was a wake-up call for me, as I couldn't stay in the same job *all* my life.

I didn't consider the good profits in our business to be a success, even though I sold millions of dollars of advertising with ease. Success for me was and always will be, to provide hope to the hopeless and to make people happy. Chocolate does just that: it brings happiness to people from all walks of life. But I was to be stuck in publishing and selling for another thirty years. And although I could sell, I never enjoyed it. It was never the real Angus Kennedy.

And so my bad luck in life continued. It was to be riddled with failures to be the real Angus for many more years, though it made me even more determined not to give in. Once you've tried for thirty years to live the dream, why stop trying?

But I really did fail at every attempt to make it and live the dream: I lost businesses. I lost a house when my wife was pregnant with our first baby. I lost all my money. I should be a plain failure, all things considered, but all these disasters, illnesses, and losses are the reason for my late success.

I almost fell into the position of a chief chocolate taster and climbed out of the Wonka branding. Britain didn't seem to have a chief of chocolate, so why not? The trick was to make the most of what I *did* have, change my perspective, and see that my thirty-year job was the only way through to uncovering my dream, or I wouldn't be there.

It was finally time to recognize that my problems were necessary steps to living and discovering what I used to think was an impossible dream, instead of seeing them as a burden and setbacks. It was as simple as that—I must never look at anything as a burden, or that would be all I would ever see and experience. It took thirty years to realize something so simple in that what you have is all you will ever need. It's perfect. But how do you land what some people tell you is the best job on the planet? Well, it's easier than you think. You almost have to stop fighting and take advantage of what you *do* have and let it propagate and allow it to happen. You need to get out of the comfort zones and get ready for change.

I believe we can each live the dream. You just need a bit of luck, to see your setbacks as foundations for your life, to be fearless, and to adopt the motto, "If you don't know you can't do it, then you can." Ignorance of how difficult it is to live the dream is a blessing! Everything we do is a step to the dream. Don't worry if you don't have it right away, you are taking the steps on the journey—even if it's a thirty-two-year one! Here's how I did it. Well firstly, it wasn't me who did it, but I allowed and accepted what was meant to be to happen.

CHAPTER 10

How to Get the Best Job in the World

Life isn't fair. It never was, and it probably never will be. Fools become celebrities and impossibly intelligent people end up on the streets begging for their next hot meal. We live in a wonky world, in which what we ignore happens and what we plan doesn't.

What I achieved isn't fair, I know. I cheated my way through school, I was a prize dropout, and yet I fly from country to country tasting goodies for the media, when there are others clearly much better suited to do it. But still it seems like a dream job and a reminder that things always get better, if only we can believe they can.

If I weren't me, I wouldn't care what a poncy chocolate taster thought of my chocolate. I wouldn't care whether it had a good snap or it was made from a single-source Ghanaian cocoa-bean farm. I certainly wouldn't read about it either. I would probably just get on with eating it. It doesn't make a product taste any better if you read about it. In fact, it probably makes the whole experience far worse.

I guess you may think, justifiably, that Britain's chief chocolate taster is nothing more than a lucky sod. You are right. But what caused my luck? You don't apply for the best jobs, because they won't really exist until you create them. Your dream vocation may not be waiting on the shelf for you. Anything on that shelf is something someone else created because *they* want you to do it for *them*. There is possibly, at least for many of us anyway, no such thing as a "dream job."

Instead, the best job in the world is the one you create for yourself to match up with your gifts. You have to carve it out from nothing. Do something you love first, and then have the guts to get on with it and hope you get paid.

Not easy, I know. We have to be brave to be a free spirit. Something that is drummed out of us for so long.

My dream job is not actually the complete dream yet. It's an example of how you can use the situation you are in to step closer to your ultimate goal, in my case helping people live their dreams—something about which I am very passionate. I am using the chocolate world, even though it looks like it's using me. I am using my situation to my advantage instead of feeling continuously suppressed by it. Just use everything you *do* have, even if you think you have nothing, as that's all you *can* do. Try not to worry about what you *don't* have. That's what I did, and that was the first step to making it and breaking out of the mold of perpetual doom.

You have to start somewhere to achieve your dream, and I want to show you how easy it is to get out there, without a logical plan and with little application of intelligence (in my case, anyway). In essence, as long as you are passionate and having a go at it, you *won't fail*.

Five years ago, there wasn't a chief chocolate taster. There were and are still a wide variety of self-proclaimed Willy Wonkas all over the place, but the chocolate industry didn't really have a cynical spokesperson. Today I do actually eat chocolate for a living and have been immersed in the industry all my life.

Fifteen years ago, I wrote down my dreams of the future in a book called *Just in Case I'm Famous*, a work of sixty thousand words in which I waxed lyrical on my hopes and aspirations. They were wild and crazy ideas and seemed impossible at the time, especially as I was broke, out of work, and had lost the family home. No, really—I truly was homeless and bankrupt.

After I helped get the business going I had decided to leave the publishing company, and subsequently I lost the family house and all my life savings after a massive failed business attempt to launch a men's magazine called *Men's Quest*. I had just about lost every penny we had when my wife was pregnant with our first child. I had to go home and tell her that the house we owned (the one that the baby was supposed to live in, complete with a lovingly prepared nursery) was going to be taken away by the bank.

Incredibly, she was okay with it. She understands, like I do, that the more money you lose, the more you can gain (hopefully sooner rather than later). It's a kind of business faith. But after putting my failed business into receivership, it was shopping in thrift stores and running around in a twenty-year-old Saab Turbo for a good while.

I wrote the book anyway. No one can stop you from dreaming. It was a powerful piece of writing, outlining my pledges for my future. In it, I told the Universe that life sucked and *this* is what I *really* want from my life. I then projected and imagined the content of that book almost daily. And guess what? Well, nothing happened, of course!

When you dream big, the goal seems impossible. But keep imagining and visualizing, all the while remaining patient. You won't get anywhere without patience. When times are bad, that's all you can do, right? It's all hoping and dreaming. It takes time. You don't win anything in the first race; you have to be able to wait the longest for the biggest prizes. All the time I was waiting, trying, failing, and pushing, I never stopped writing, ever.

Nothing happened for far too long. I suffered endless frustrations and letdowns and then, in 2011, I met a journalist from the *Times* newspaper who wanted to write an article on the biscuit industry, and he needed an expert in a position of authority on the subject. He found himself in front of me by chance in Cologne, at the show I first went to at the age of ten. We only started talking because I went up to him at the trade show and had a chat with him, asking if he was enjoying the exhibition.

I always go up and speak to people first; it's one of the things I learned to do well at school. If you believe life has an opportunity, even when life sucks, then you talk to everyone, as one day you *will* get the right person. If you think life is doomed, then you talk to no one and life is most certainly doomed.

To my surprise, I found that, after a life in the industry, I knew everything about the companies he wanted to include, and I whizzed off quotes and data with ease.

For the first time, my name appeared in the *Times*, which I found most refreshing. I thought nothing of it other than a nice thing to show my wife over a glass of cheap chardonnay in the evening.

After it was published, the media took interest in me. Gradually more newspapers got in touch, looking for new angles on the industry. I found the entire experience quite enjoyable, chatting away to reporters and answering *their* questions for a change on anything from shrinkflation to the cocoa shortage story and whether the world will run out of chocolate.

The media is always on the lookout for new "characters." Enter Angus Kennedy, a manic dad who slugs down chocolate all day long and does nothing else whatsoever. He doesn't even get overweight. I couldn't stop them. The might of the *Daily Mail* and the *Sun* came on board, running full-page profiles on me, and headlines appeared saying "Willy Wonka Eat Your Heart Out" and so forth.

And then the *Daily Star* did a feature on chocolate and fertility. Bingo! Having five kids in tow made another great story. Before too long, Angus Kennedy had appeared in the *Guardian*, the *Telegraph*, the *Times*, and nearly all the nationals, plus radio stations up and down the country and, soon after, national TV and Al Jazeera TV in Washington. Finally, the last prophecy of my strange visitor to number 22 all those years ago started to grind into motion. But it's by no means complete.

You may ask what did I do to deserve or achieve all this recognition. Angus Kennedy, the failure no less, seemed to be doing okay at last. We were and still are not especially rich, with five kids, but I went from being bankrupt to a $1.3 million house and a job to die for within ten years. Was my success partly because I wrote a book predicting my future? I think it might actually have had a big effect.

———

All my failures seemed to spark even more interest from the media. I was almost grateful for them. A rags-to-riches story—they loved it. I must admit, the headlines that portrayed a man that went from being broke to the King of Chocolate was a great seller. Both newspapers and tabloids kept coming back for more, helped greatly by offerings of free-at-any-time-to-journalists chocolate.

The media loves to create characters that allow us to imagine that there are people who can just sit in a café on a low income, like J. K. Rowling was reported to do, and become, overnight, one of the most successful authors of the century.

And that applied to me, too. I was the British chocolate-tasting cynic and total dropout who went from being uneducated, unemployed, and bankrupt, with no qualifications, to an up-and-coming celebrity and chocolate king. I think celebrities often find their rise to fame just as curious as their followers do. I agree, it's not fair, but it's fate, albeit assisted by my imagination. Fate needs igniting. A dream fuels it all, so never stop dreaming, okay?

The press is the most powerful tool available, and they simply didn't listen to any of the dull aspects of my life. I also changed the diapers, moaned about income tax, and emptied the dishwasher, but they needed a character to help their readers believe that they could also have a job like Angus Kennedy and gobble up lavish amounts of chocolate whilst spread out finely over a chaise from morning till dusk. I went with it.

Whether I liked it or not, there was a good reason why I could tell the *Times* details they most likely hadn't heard about the confectionery industry in years. It was simply that I had spent my whole life learning about sweets. Curiously, it does seem that fate is inescapable once you let it out of your bag. If you are not destined to pass an exam, you won't. If you *are* destined to stay in a small, uneventful publishing company in Kent without knowing why until you are fifty years old, you will. Accepting your position, no matter how bad it may be, provides freedom. Faith is knowing that there are good reasons for what we thought were bad things.

And so, over a period of ten years practicing my imagination techniques and positive thinking, I got myself onto television by imagining it every morning. What else could I do when facing the impossible (like getting onto television at fifty years old while going gray and being unable to read a menu if it's dark)?

"You're having a laugh," friends said. "Who wants a knackered old dad of five struggling to live the dream in the UK?"

But if you make a decision, make a pledge, stick at it for years, and don't listen to anyone but yourself, then you will have already succeeded, because it *will* happen.

Interestingly, I have read articles that claim we have on average sixty thousand thoughts a day. Some scientists claim we think 90 percent of the same thoughts the next day. So, if you wonder why life is not changing and you're thinking the same things that you thought yesterday, then you shouldn't be so surprised that life today is pretty much what you thought it would be yesterday. We think our futures, which then become reality.

Just change what you think. Swap a few negatives to a few positives to feel your aspirations—and that's the basics. That's how I did it when in fact I should be a drug addict, dead, or clinically depressed. But we have to take every opportunity that comes our way, even if we fail, because failure leads to something.

I continued to help countless TV show researchers with their ideas for chocolate programs, to make them rock for their producers, even though I never appeared on the programs or got paid. I offered myself for unpaid interviews in difficult hours and wrote free articles for papers, toiling late into the evenings until my wife almost deserted me. I did this for many years.

I took calls from the press and radio on holiday (in secret), and some nights I would work until 3:00 a.m., talking to syndicated radio shows one after the other. Never once was I paid, and I always put 100 percent into every assignment that came my way.

I consistently sent the journalists I worked with chocolates afterward (a treat always helps). Every time I went on a film set or on a TV show, I made sure that just about everyone, from the producer to the runner to the soundman, had some chocolate to munch on throughout the shoot. And if I forgot one member of the team, which I could because I am fifty after all, I would certainly know about it!

Keep giving all the time and keep being friendly to everyone, even though you think you get nothing back, even if you have a fake publicist, an ineffective PR person, or even a fake literary agent like I suffered in the past. You are entering into a new industry and you *will* be nibbled by the sharks. They like to keep you alive so they can nibble again, so you never die.

Making it in TV is like walking through the woods, eating all the poisonous mushrooms, coming out alive, and wanting to eat more poison. You have to keep going on and on when you think you are heading nowhere. Keep going, keep walking, keep falling, and keep getting up when you should be down, and don't listen to anyone but yourself. You will succeed. You can't see it, but you know it, so you *have* to get up and keep going.

A lifetime of hard work and frustrations isn't so bad if the prize is right. If you don't stop trying, you have succeeded. Failure is stopping, sitting down, and doing nothing.

The dream is yours, or you wouldn't dream it, right? I was told I was mad, but I succeeded in imagining failing my way to becoming a success. Be human and use your imagination to change.

Through a chance meeting and my knowledge of an industry, I became known as the chief chocolate taster. Getting to be something like a chocolate taster is not actually that hard. It's nothing spectacular either. I mean, it's not as if I'm saving any lives just yet or sitting in my private mansion in Barbados.

But you can be what you want to be. Start by writing it down. Believe it, pledge it, imagine it, expect it, and get up and keep failing at it. But don't set yourself completely on it as the final goal, as success often happens in between the failures you plan. Think about what will make you truly happy. Be prepared to change course, fail, and be derailed at any moment.

Get yourself nice and comfortable now, because I'm going to take you on a journey into the magical world of chocolate. Is it a pleasure or a curse? What is it like to be a chocolate taster and have an expense account to buy all the candy you could wish for? What is it like having *loads* of chocolate at hand, pretty much all day, every day? And will our chocolate run out? Why am I not five miles wide? And, wait for it, I have a terrible secret to which I have not yet confessed—I can't get rid of the chocolate. Read on and I'll tell you where it goes and why I can't even throw it away.

CHAPTER 11

Goods to Confess

I receive a lot of chocolates, I confess. Last week, for example, I was invited to Southern Italy to see an Italian company positioned, like a fairy tale edifice, right on top of a beautiful mountain in the Tyrolean Alps. It is one of the biggest companies specializing in wafers and chocolate products in the world, producing 877 million items a year, 1,000 tons of goodies every single day. I toured the high-tech factory with the owner, who offered me his delicious and crispy chocolate wafers right from the conveyor belts as we chatted about his business.

After a twenty-four-hour trip, I returned through London's Heathrow Airport customs with several bags of chocolate swinging from my fingers and bulging out of my hand luggage. Customs should ask me for "goods to confess" instead of "goods to declare." I always take an empty suitcase, just in case. And excuse the pun, but you would be nuts to leave no space in your suitcase when visiting places like this magnificent plant that produces up to 41 tons of chocolate and wafers in a single hour.

This time my initial hoard wasn't enough. The Italian business I visited loved my story, and an exceedingly large box the size of an antique Victorian butler sink arrived in my office to say thanks. The delivery was packed to the brim with even more delicious Italian chocolates and wafers. I brought some home, too. If you were to sit with me for dinner, we would not even find room for our plates, as the kitchen table is often completely and evenly covered with these chocolate products. I have to push them aside to make way for my laptop.

And in my office—not the one at home—I also have some Storck Werther's Toffees to try, some Ferrero Rocher sent directly from their UK office, and a wonderful Peruvian chocolate-tasting kit with different percentages of Peruvian cocoa for each product. Oh, and there's that prototype chocolate bar from an English flavor company. Each segment you break off the bar tastes different. Clever stuff, and another first I believe.

Then there are those white peach and tequila sunrise–flavored biscuits from a flavor lab in Germany that I am due to visit next month—they have never been tried before (apparently). Then, next week, I will be the first person in the UK to try a hot chocolate that has been de-bittered with coca leaf extracts from Peru and Bolivia. (Coca is where cocaine comes from, but the hot chocolate is narcotic-free.)

The guy from Peru is coming straight over from the coca fields (through the same customs as me) with his coca leaf–sweetened chocolate with no sugar. I hope he gets through, because, if he does, I will be trying the world's first chocolate flavored with coca.

I was also one of the first to try raw flavanols imported from Belgium, which came in on the Eurostar this time, across the Channel. Flavanols are found within the cocoa bean. They are a type of polyphenol (didn't mean much to me either at first), but they are a broad group of natural compounds found in plants. Many polyphenols, including flavanols, play a protective role for plants and when we consume them, it's believed and reported that they have an antioxidant effect for us too. There are many different types of flavanols. The flavanols found in cacao include catechins and tannins. Both of these are also found in tea. Catechins are thought to be responsible for the health benefits of green tea.

They can be destroyed by heat, so when chocolate is heated during processing, these flavanols and their unique properties are very often lost. This company has extracted the flavanols without heating the chocolate, to make a pure powder. They have also recently made claims that the flavanols "could increase your blood flow and circulation." It is said that Casanova used to take a cocoa drink, cold, three or four times a day, to boost his "activities."

Two journalists from two of the world's most read newspapers and I ended up in a rather posh hotel in London to test the products with a representative of the company that produces the flavanol powder. We were to be the first to drink this raw flavanol miracle. I was praying that it wouldn't be too powerful.

We all gulped down the rather bitter product and sat in the hotel bar waiting for the "Casanova effect" to kick in—and all in the name of journalism.

It didn't taste that nice, but thinking of the effect was all-consuming. I waited, they waited, we laughed, they talked, and we asked each other questions, professionally, like journalists would do. Did it have an effect on me? Of course not! Is it any surprise that I am so cynical? But it was definitely worth trying.

By the way, if you're looking for the Casanova effect, I would suggest a bottle of French Mumm rosé champagne and some Pink Marc de Champagne Truffles from Charbonnel et Walker on London's Bond Street.

We finished the meeting in the name of journalism, laughing and looking forward to my crazy "next stunt" with the press. Chocolate might increase blood flow, but then again, for me at least, I can't tell if it did or didn't. I don't think I really needed it, given that I was in a hotel bar with such attractive company.

I returned home that evening and my wife asked how work had been that day. I told her the whole story. She raised her eyebrows in approval and carried on peeling a zucchini for the evening's bolognaise. She had heard it all before.

I really do receive a lot of chocolates and candy now, and to top it all, I have a personal candy expense credit card. What that means is that *in the name of research*, of course, just in case I don't have enough goodies piling up, I can walk right into any supermarket on a whim, pull out the corporate card, and buy any candy. Okay, I guess anyone can do that, but for me it's part of the job that has to be done. I can go and buy anything, even if I have had it before. All in the name of journalistic ideas.

Recently, as I run a major chocolate business conference in London, I was able to buy champagne on a try-before-you-buy basis. The event (the London Chocolate Forum) draws more than three hundred of the top chocolatiers from across the world, so naturally I had to sample the champagne for them. Again, this was on the corporate card. It is at this point that my wife immediately puts down the zucchini peeler and we both race to the nearest Waitrose to try the next champagne sample.

Free champagne and free chocolate—yes, it's a pretty cool job. If I carry on, I am going to have another murder attempt on my life, as people might just get a little too jealous. Champagne and chocolate mean another thing, too: more babies. One more kid and you won't need to murder me. Sex is great for having babies, but having babies is terrible for having sex.

I also buy things I haven't seen before and *have* to try, like Japanese giant hornet honey, for example. You drink the "honey," which, supposedly, includes secreted juices extracted from the body of the hornet. You're not supposed to eat the hornet, thank God. The Japanese hornet is said to possess the greatest endurance of any living creature. Just thirty of these flying grim reapers can destroy thirty thousand poor bees in just four hours, so the idea is that you become super-human when consuming these strange insect juices. Nice marketing, but I just felt a little sick and glad the hornet was dead.

On the subject of bugs, I have another product on my desk, in case I feel the urge: chocolate shots. A chocolate shot comes ready in a plastic toy syringe; you inject a chocolate and ground insect paste directly into your mouth. I did try it. It wasn't actually that bad. I haven't seen a huge number in the shops yet, though.

I also make my own chocolate-covered locusts and mealworms, as I have a mini-chocolate tempering machine at home. I buy the bugs frozen, fry them, caramelize them, and add a little mint and blackberry essence donated from a friend of mine who is a professional flavorist. Then, of course, I cover them all in chocolate. They're so good that I was asked to go on ITV's *Food Glorious Food* and present them to Tom Parker Bowles, whom I discovered is connected to the British royal family. He wasn't supposed to know what they were, and he tried them while I waited. He crunched on the chocolate bugs, asking me what they were, with the cameras on us waiting for the reaction. I am not sure if he liked them, but he enjoyed the surprise and, like anyone connected to the royal family, was exquisitely polite about it.

We should eat more bugs, entomophagy makes much more sense than eating meat. Research says that ounce for ounce, crickets provide more than twice the protein of beef. Plus, tests say that crickets have nearly five times as much magnesium as beef and nearly all the essential amino acids. And around 30 percent of the land on Earth is being used for pasture to grow food to feed livestock that we then eat. It doesn't make sense to me to clear forest for that. Insects can be raised using much less water and energy than traditional livestock, and they emit a fraction of the greenhouse gases. All makes sense, but people just don't like the idea at the moment, as we haven't looked at ways of processing our bugs. Though a nice Dominican Republic cocoa chocolate covering sure helps!

Another strange invention that was brought to my attention is a French product called Le Whif, or something to that effect. The idea is: you no longer need to *eat* chocolate to experience it—instead, you just inhale it, and supposedly it has the same sensation as eating it. It is a spray of very fine cocoa powder that you sniff, and then you never need to eat chocolate or put on weight again. I *did* eat chocolate again, but I leave it to you to judge which pastime you would prefer.

Bordering on the supremely ridiculous, I managed to get hold of a kind of anti-stage-fright chocolate from Germany. No kidding! It comes in a blister pack, like your pain medication does. You take a pill-shaped chocolate from the pack, and it helps you "battle against daily stresses" including, among other ailments, stage fright. Which, of course, we all have every day, don't we? I've now seen it all. I propose there be a national day of no-we-are-not-complete-idiots.

I get to try a lot of cool stuff, but I don't just gulp it down like those pelicans swallow live pigeons in St. James's Park near Buckingham Palace. There is a kind of science to it, believe it or not.

There is a professional way to test chocolate that isn't just eating it and saying, "yeah, yummy" (though it's very tempting). You have to look at the surface of the product: is it shiny or not (the latter being better)? Is it smooth, or are there any bubbles on the surface? What does it smell like? When you break it, does it bend or snap (the snap being what you want)? Is it smooth and not gritty when you eat it? Smooth is generally better, though chocolate in the US is deliberately grittier with a larger particle size. Does it melt or kind of go sludgy when you pop it in your mouth, meaning the fats are cheaper? Can you actually taste the chocolate, or is it just sweet? Close your eyes.

I eat some chocolate that is so sweet I can't taste the chocolate. And then there's the taste of the bean; you can absolutely taste a good cocoa bean, and the beans can be hugely different.

Being surrounded by sweets has its problems. A lot of people who have worked for me could get larger by the month, my teeth need attention all the time, and I can never give chocolate to anyone as a gift, as they think I haven't spent anything on them. Oh, and I have a problem getting rid of chocolate. It's a unique problem, I admit, and one with which I don't think anyone else really has to cope, but I genuinely can't get rid of the stuff.

Chocolate builds up on my desk and at home, in my workbag, next to my bed, in the kitchen drawers, the garage. It's everywhere. I am a pretty amazing dad to have. All my kids' friends say to them, "Your dad really has the best job in the world, when can we come round?" But it's still everywhere.

The event I founded with my company four years ago, the London Chocolate Forum, is now becoming a sizable chocolate event for the international industry. And guess what? *It's full of chocolate*. Many attendees leave their products behind, as they travel from abroad, and ask us if we can help find a nice home for them. I am talking about some of the finest Belgian, French, Swiss, German, English, and Italian chocolates in the world, made to exhibition standards.

This year I ended up with a sculptured chocolate tree in my office that I needed to find a home for. Last year, no kidding, we had several chocolate bars weighing at least 22 pounds each. They were absolutely huge—I mean taller and wider than my five-year-old son. He could not even transport one to his secret eating location (normally under the piano, so not such a secret). He was unable to get his teeth over it to bite it, either, which was very funny. Even if he had managed to dislocate his jaw, it was too thick to cut through with mere teeth. You needed to jump on this monster bar or hit it with a large rolling pin to get a decent chunk off. And apart from my personal consumption and those around me, I have to find willing homes for it all. You would think it would be the easiest thing in the world to do. People, you would have thought, would grab chocolate off you faster than you would swat a rhinoceros botfly sitting on your forearm preparing to feast.

Distributing free chocolate is tough because many people are suspicious and think it's too good to be true. Similarly, if you gave someone a few $10 bills in the street, they would wonder why.

A very long time ago in the early 1980s, my company ran a mock sweetshop. We invited schoolchildren to come in and buy sweets with fake money, and we analyzed what they bought in comparison to what they said they would buy before they entered the shop.

I asked a few companies (some multinationals) if they would like to participate, and they loved the idea. The first delivery arrived from a huge Nestlé container truck, so big that it didn't fit down the mews to our office door. We had to walk the pallet, which was taller and wider than I was, along the pavement. Then there were several more pallets. The survey went well, but it was probably the largest amount of chocolate, biscuits, and candy that we have ever had at any time in our office. We couldn't even get to our desks.

After a few days of feeling imprisoned by chocolates, I threw some candies out the window as a joke, saying I just couldn't get rid of the stuff. I didn't think much of it, but I heard the distant voices of a few kids outside the office and, to my delight, the candy disappeared.

The next day, I did the same, thinking the women who used to hang out drinking in the street outside our office door would also dig in. Again, the sweets rather satisfactorily disappeared—and very efficiently, too. Pleased with my new distribution techniques, I continued the process for several days.

Then I went abroad and was away from the office for a couple days. When I returned to the street, about a hundred yards away from the office door, I could hear chanting and screaming. I thought there was a demonstration, as we were close to the Finsbury Park Mosque, where there was trouble at that time. To my horror, I realized there were several hundred children (and their parents) all chanting, "Sweets, sweets, we want more sweets."

The whole school and neighborhood had heard of the street that rained candy; the nice man will give us all candy. I had to call the police in the end, as I couldn't get into my own office without being mobbed. Ha! When the police arrived, even they asked if we had any sweets for them. I obliged willingly, and it seemed to solve the whole thing right away. If I threw sweets to kids today, I would be arrested.

———————

My greatest occupational hazard is weight gain, though. In fact, the question I get asked the most, after "How the hell did you get *that* job?" and "Will our chocolate run out?" is, "Why, Angus, are you not the size of a bus?" I developed a technique to combat the extra calories, which I never thought about sharing until now. I should be well over two hundred pounds, so here's how I manage my weight.

CHAPTER 12

Weight Control

I'm not aware of a single diet book that my wife has read that she says has actually worked for her. What I am about to write may not work for you either. However, what I do appears to work for me, at least. I am living evidence—the world's leading chocolate expert is as slim as a rake.

So how do I do it?

Well, first off, I have to get to my mind before the food industry does.

The first stage of any battle is to learn about the opponent, which in this case is a formidable player. This is a fight between a multi-billion-dollar food and drink industry and a human being trying to eat healthy food. Unfortunately, that healthy food is comparatively expensive and difficult to find. The cheapest foods tend to have the largest amount of fats, sugars, and cheap ingredients.

The less we know about what goes into our food, the more an industry can make claims that we swallow without question. We have become hypnotized by a sea of inappropriate marketing claims, and often we witness the absurd use of the word "healthy."

Isn't it about time we changed all that?

The food industry spends billions to prove that something that could be bad for you is good and then invests the same again into studying the psychology of our purchasing habits when we stop buying something.

So, let's not be surprised that so many of us are now overweight. Through availability and marketing, we've been conditioned to believe that a 64-ounce double-gulp fizzy drink sounds like a great idea. We don't even question that it's an astoundingly unnatural product this size, with up to 7.4 ounces of pure sugar and more than 700 calories. We have accepted the unacceptable. We even think National Cheeseburger Day makes sense, when it's the most farcical idea we could possibly conjure up, *ever*. What utter nonsense.

We think it's normal that Halloween is now about buying buckets of sweets and dishing them out to the neighbors, while hardly saying hello. Christmas and Valentine's Day are in hot pursuit of the game, fast becoming events on which to eat more and more confectionery and absorb less and less spiritual meaning about the festivals themselves. The food industry is converting days and events that go back thousands of years into nothing more than sugar-crazed feeding sessions. I recently read a UK survey that revealed, when children in London were asked what Easter is about, more than 60 percent felt it was about eating chocolate, with no reference to Jesus.

It's logical that we are in trouble when we consider the astonishingly large amounts of junk food available to eat in the world, how *easy* it is to come across it, and how easy it has become for companies to promote it at every juncture of our lives.

Recently I was at Universal Studios in California, one of my favorite attractions, with all the kids on a family holiday. I love that place, but it seemed that everywhere we turned we saw fast-food outlets and shops offering for sale huge amounts of candy, cakes, and burgers. People were sitting down just about everywhere I looked, eating and munching everything from lollipops the size of side plates, to ice-cream portions that were so big our entire family bought one to share (for seven people), and even then we had to leave some. I saw children sitting on walls, munching their way through giant Homer Simpson donuts (must have at least five hundred calories each) with what seemed to be bucket-sized sugary drinks. The portion sizes, in my opinion, were completely insane.

Theme parks all over the world seem to have become havens to have an excuse to gorge on huge cookies, chocolate cakes, burgers, chips, and fries—this type of food is everywhere. Parents buy this stuff for their kids, though, so what hope do the kids have later in life? They will think it's normal to buy it for their own kids. Perhaps thin people will soon be a thing of the past.

The park seemed to be a giant eating fest as people waited for rides as opposed to running around and having an energetic day out with the kids. Isn't the whole point to burn some energy, go on rides, have fun, and run about? Not anymore, it seems. Wherever we go now, eating is fast becoming the primary attraction.

The food industry and governments have both played a major part in creating this problem and only recently realized the fingers are pointing at them. Do we really need super-sized donuts and bucket-sized sugary drinks that are so heavy you can't lift them off the table? Is it okay to have hot chocolates with more calories than chocolate bars?

Why can't the addition of sugar be regulated far more? There are no limits in portion size, which in my view is a big mistake. Portion sizes are totally abnormal, and even a common Dutch Holstein cow would struggle to burn off the calories humans consume in some daily diets.

At some point in our evolution, we have to begin the journey back to what humans should actually eat and should always have eaten. But again, we are being controlled most brilliantly by an industry. If we ate healthier, it would put many gigantic food companies out of business. The consequences of us all being healthy would be monumentally *unhealthy* for the food industry and tax incomes. That's what we are up against. They survive or we do, but not both. So they pretend that the foods they sell us are actually healthy.

Let's start by understanding that it's very difficult to go into a shop and avoid unhealthy food. However, we can at least start to use our imagination and understand why we are doing what we are doing and why it's so difficult to stop. We just have to start with the mind and not go on another flipping diet that won't work anyway, as we've tried that before. You can't cure your body of toxins without curing your mind of the toxins first.

No one, apart from you and me, needs us to stop eating empty calories. Knowing that fact is the first step.

Having been very keen on rowing in the past and rowing to international standards, I love running or rowing for long distances. Unfortunately, I had a knee operation recently, so I am writing in an office and can't get to the gym. This is therefore not so much about a workout, but *working it out.*

One of my techniques is to use my brain, and not just for filling it up like a sponge by watching TV, gawking at an iPhone, or any other passive brain exercise requiring minimal intelligence, such as flicking through nonsense on Facebook or tuning into the lives of people you're not really interested in. You need to challenge your brain and think hard. I am always ravenous when writing and engaging in this writing.

The brain is said to use up more calories per pound than anything else in the body. To most people, 1.5 calories per minute might not seem much, but your brain accounts for just 2 percent of your body weight and yet burns up to 20 percent, three hundred to four hundred of the two thousand calories the average person needs per day. Put it this way: your brain can burn up three average-sized chocolate bars a day. It's a great fat burner. And its primary source of fuel is said to be glucose!

I have been writing for six hours since I got back from work, and my brain has probably already gobbled up a Dairy Milk chocolate bar—all while just sitting here writing and not going to the gym. I've tricked my mind with a sugar-free candy to replace the candy I would have eaten otherwise. It's 10:00 p.m. as I write this, and I'm sucking on a sugar-free Werther's Original apple-flavored candy from Germany. It's a nice candy, by the way.

The key is to look at it this way: think of the time you would need and what you would need to do to burn off the calories you're considering consuming.

That's how I stay at my weight. I mentally convert the food I eat into the hours of exercise required to burn it all off. I imagine what extra physical effort I would have to do to burn off the calories. Time taken to burn off the carbs, though difficult to quantify, is something that is conveniently missing from most of our food labels.

Let's say I have a can of Coke before bed, lounge on the couch, and watch TV. That fizzy drink has approximately 138 calories. Sugary drinks as a category, it's reported, now account for more calorie intake than all the confectionery in the US, so sugary drinks are often a worse culprit than the sweets. I would have to get up off the couch and play badminton for around 15 minutes to burn off my Coke.

Or, let's say I have a chocolate bar as an evening snack after dinner. To burn it off, according to some websites, I would have to walk constantly up my steep old Victorian servants' staircase for one hour. In an ideal world, it would be a lot easier not eating it. Start by understanding the effort required to burn off what you're about to eat. You just need to start thinking and being aware of what you're feeding your body. But be patient.

Get your mind working on your diet first. Ignore all the advertisements for fast food and foods that are high in sugars, and then ask yourself, preferably while you hold the package in the supermarket before you buy it, "What does my body need to do to work off this food?"

———————

I recently went to a fruit-processing plant in Poland and was informed that Coca-Cola's approximate 1.4 ounces of sugar per can is actually less than some apple drinks, so it's not just fizzy drinks you have to watch. In fact, some so-called fruit drinks score a massive 165 calories for the same amount of fluid. We are hoodwinked into believing they are healthy by reading the word "fruit" on the package.

There's something not right here. You can take any product and add iron and claim it's "high in iron," or add fiber or vitamin C, for example, and lead people to believe it's healthy, merely by focusing on that one ingredient that might make it a tiny bit beneficial. With this logic, you could add iron to the cardboard box that your cereal comes in and claim it healthy, too.

The same goes for chocolate. Marketers ignore how fattening it really is by focusing on the benefit of antioxidants. There are hundreds of antioxidants, but the human body, it's reported, can only absorb a handful of them. Many are of little value. Cocoa does contain the antioxidants catechins and procyanidins, which are said to be of benefit to our health.

But careful what you read. Larger quantities, they say, make no difference to your diet. Therefore, a product high in antioxidants probably isn't as big a deal as we may have thought. The Cochrane review from 2008 demonstrated that antioxidant supplements actually seem to increase mortality

Chocolate is for pleasure. Just stay healthy so you can eat it, not the other way around. If you want antioxidants, then why not eat a walnut?

The word *diet* itself is misleading, as it basically means, in my dictionary anyway, "the kind of food one habitually eats." So we are all on diets—it's just another word for eating what we eat. Forget about *being on a diet*, because the only way then to lose weight, logically, is *not to be on a diet* and not eat what you habitually eat.

It's another bit of marketing spin: go on a diet, come this way, and buy all this extra diet food to help you lose weight. If you think about it, it's absurd.

Now look at what we are up against. Most of our food intake is loaded with sugar already, through our normal habitual foods of salad dressings, sauces, breads, cereals, fruit juices, and so on. We have been fighting a losing battle, as we have been eating added sugars without really knowing it for years on end.

The global food industry is mysteriously quiet about the volumes of sugar they include in our produce. Look at the labels on the ingredients of your processed food and you'll see that few products don't contain glucose syrups or sugar. Hidden sugars can be found in almost all processed foods. Some cereals, in my opinion, should not even be called cereal, as they are blatant confectionery products. Kellogg's Honey Smacks, for example, are sweets in my opinion, but they're marketed as a breakfast cereal even though they are reported to have up to 55 percent sugar. That's not right.

Look at it another way: if you add more alcohol to wine, at some stage it legally must be called a spirit, but if you keep adding sugar to bread, it's still called bread. This needs addressing urgently through new labeling.

It's widely reported that 80 percent of *all* food bought in UK supermarkets has added sugar, and the US figure is similar at just under 80 percent (of six hundred thousand products). Sugar tastes good, and it's cheap and easy to work with, as it bulks up food (it makes it bigger and makes the product hold its shape, too).

So it's not your fault if you can't lose weight, okay? You're pumping in sugar all the time, with no idea you're doing it. Producers often deliberately put sugar in food because not only is it cheap, it will make you buy it again and again. There is a good reason.

If you eat a lot of sugar, it's very likely you are addicted to it. You're also contributing handsomely to an estimated $97 billion global sweetener industry. Now, no one in government or high up in industry is going to want to stop you from eating it, are they? I hope I am wrong. Sugar sadly seems to be all about profit.

Research published by PLOS ONE in August 2007 highlighted an experiment "involving rats deciding between intense sweetness and cocaine. The rats were given cocaine until they became dependent on it. Then, researchers provided them a choice: the rats could continue to be high as kites munching through the cocaine or switch to an intense sweet taste. And guess which one the rodents chose? Well, the study found that 94 percent of the rats chose to make the switch to the sweet product, which I find remarkable. Even when they had to work harder to access the sweeter reward, it's claimed. So don't try to cut yourself up when you reach for the sweet stuff in the aisles. You may be addicted, and maybe I am too! But it's my job to eat it. We all do strange things for money.

I recently watched a very good film, *Fed Up*, predicting that by 2050, one third of all Americans will have diabetes. I believe sugar is addictive. I know I have seen kids addicted to it, my daughter was, for example. She could not stop eating sugar, and in the end, we had to get help. But there wasn't any, no one cared a hoot. Eating disorders are conveniently brushed aside. We overcame it together in the end. I read a load of books about sugar addiction and eating disorders, and she cured herself with a lot of support from Mum and Dad.

If you are a food executive and you want to sell more of your products and get people to like them, easy, put sugar in them. Sugar, by the way, is the cheapest ingredient in chocolate and in most cases, other foods. Great! We have a solution: put more and more in, get people addicted, and then reap the financial rewards. You have a cheap product to make while the world gets more obese, and who cares, anyway? You are rich and everyone else is doing it too.

Well it's *not* okay, but there's too much money at stake to change. Very slowly we are seeing more sugar-free options in confectionery, and I commend the producers pioneering these products. But artificial sweeteners can be another problem; look up the history of aspartame, for example. Some say it should never have been approved by the FDA. I am on an aspartame-free diet now, by the way. I never touch it.

Wherever possible we should try to avoid the *hidden sugars*, the ones of which we might not be aware, but that's tough. It's very hard to buy sugar-free. It seems to be either too trendy to buy, or five times the price of "normal" sugar-based items.

These studies on the harmful effects of sugar pop up from time to time, but generally they do not make people change their views. In my thirty-year career as editor of the world's biggest authority on the subject, never once have I received a press release stating the addictive qualities of sugar.

That may be how it is today, but things are starting to change. Even my kids are looking at the sugar per one hundred grams on the cereal packages in the morning. I gave up cereal a few years ago, and now try and have a piece of fruit for breakfast instead. I am moving away from processed foods in general anyway.

A "health bar," sometimes called a sports bar, often has more calories than a chocolate wafer bar. What's that got to do with health or sports? It's fair enough if we are living in a croft on a small island off the Scottish coast, the weather has destroyed our crops, we are starving, and we need it, but I never ate sports bars when I rowed for my country.

And then there is a pint of beer, say a pint of Stella Artois, which is quoted at around 244 calories—more than a reasonably sized portion of chocolate cake. Alcohol contains seven calories per gram, which is second only to fat, which has nine calories per gram. Sugar, incidentally, has only four calories per gram, so let's give it a little credit here: alcohol and fat are more fattening than sugar. However, mix them up to make a product like brandy butter, which is all three, and you have a huge dose of calories per gram, and curiously it seems to be these foods that people crave the most. Alcohol, however, seems to have escaped the radar somewhat.

Many people can easily drink four pints of beer, which can be at least 900 calories in one sitting. Burning that off is serious exercise: running up the stairs, nonstop, for one hour. I can't see many blokes doing that after the pub. If the pub was five miles from home and they ran all the way home, that would be another way of doing it.

I tend only to drink wine, as I know there are fewer calories, but even a 250-milliliter glass of wine still contains roughly 225 calories, some of which are very sweet and are roughly the equivalent of a 44-gram bar of chocolate. If you really want to hit the calories, though, try a double piña colada with rum, which depending on its size of course, can weigh in at more than 500 calories, not far from that of a Big Mac or six 45-gram chocolate bars (the size roughly of a Cadbury's Dairy Milk).

I was on a sugar-free lifestyle for four months from Christmas to Easter last year, and I can tell you it's hard work. It is hard because it's almost impossible to eat anything without sugar, and it's not yet socially acceptable to refuse food with sugar in it, since people think you are mad or trying to be trendy or awkward. The most difficult aspect was eating out, as how can you tell if what's on the menu has sugar in it without asking the waiter to ask the chef?

I tried on a couple of occasions to ask in restaurants and then simply got around it by not ordering anything with sauces, toppings, and so on. Work was interesting, as my job is to eat sweets, so it was a bit of a daft thing to do, but I had a lot of support and many producers sent me their sugar-free products so I could test them out.

Sugar-free candies are increasingly available and the industry and some governments at last are actually trying hard now, to address the balance, but sugar-free is not readily available in supermarkets. I know some producers that are making sugar-free candies, lollipops, chocolate bars, and other ingenious products, reporting them to be the fastest growing sector for their confectionery companies. The confectionery industry is not to be blamed as much as other industries. We know sweets are usually made with sugar. It's an honest industry.

It's cheaper to sell confectionery and food with sugar than with artificial sweeteners, so the decision to do so seems to be about profit at the expense of our waistlines. But I do believe opinions are changing and the industry is trying, though it's not happening fast enough. The food industry could take out vast quantities of sugar from processed food and that would help considerably.

But would you give your partner a box of sugar-free chocolates for Valentine's Day? They might say, "Are you saying I'm fat?" and throw the box at your face. So, it's often the case that the most successful sugar-free products don't advertise that they are sugar-free. It's just the policy of the company not to provide so much sugar.

Fat makes up around 50 percent of a chocolate bar's ingredients, while sugar pretty much accounts for the other half. The fat in chocolate can be replaced with certain emulsifiers to reduce the calorie intake by up to 20 percent. It's expensive to do, but it can be done. But why bother? Collectively, a manufacturer can currently reduce a chocolate bar's calories by up to 40 percent, but it costs more money to do it. It's easier to make the product smaller and keep the same recipe. There are also new methods coming from South America that can make a chocolate product that does not have any sugar or fat at all. The industry is too slow in my opinion to embrace this right now, but I believe huge changes are on the way.

However, ultimately, until recently, you always needed to have fat to hold the chocolate together, so there have only been a few producers that could make their chocolate this way. Furthermore, you have to have cocoa butter in the chocolate or it can't legally be called chocolate.

———————

There are some days when I really do eat candy all day, so I've had to work out a system. To compensate for today's candy intake, for example, I had a cup of tea and an orange for breakfast and went to the gym at lunchtime for a half-hour swim.

Eating smaller meals and exercising puts me in calorie debt. I don't advise this really, but it's what *I* do. It works for me, and answers the question as to why I am still the same 170 pounds I was twenty years ago.

Yesterday, however, I ate like a pig. Then again, it doesn't matter, as some days I eat a lot but generally I think about how long it takes to burn it off. It really can work for you, if you train your mind to think first.

There is nothing worse than sitting at your desk at work while everyone else is scarfing down tasty sandwiches, or worse still, being tempted by a gang that is going to eat out. They think you are unwell if you don't eat with them, and it's not worth the hassle. I take myself out of the equation every now and then during my lunch break at work and do something else for an hour, so I can't smell or see any food that I did not plan to eat. Then I have the small snack I brought with me when I get back to my desk and it's then too late to get anything else.

I also know what quantity of sugars I eat. Information that is on the packets is hugely useful, stating on nearly all products the sugar content per one hundred grams. Some cereals, like Cocoa Pops, I believe, are more than 30 percent sugar. That's not staple food in my opinion—that's too much sugar for me. I try to stay under ten grams per one hundred grams of sugar or not eat it at all. Everything from gherkins to pickled herrings can be loaded with sugar, and often they don't say how much, which is another big problem.

So you sign up for a gym, which is great. But I see people from the gym having a beer after a workout, maybe two more pints of beer and a health/muesli bar. That's on average 208 calories per beer and 190 calories for the "health bar." They just shoved down over 800 calories after their gym trip and no way did some of them do the five-mile run needed to burn it off. Consequently, a gym isn't necessarily the answer, as it often just makes you feel better (you are doing something) and helps you think you are healthy or winning a losing battle. You might actually be better off meditating, thinking, and doing nothing at all instead, as long as you don't hit the fattening foods.

Many of the gym folk keep wearing the tracksuit after the gym session, to make themselves believe they are fitter and slimmer while they sip the pints and eat fried foods. Many don't do much aerobic work at all, so they probably burn 300 calories at best walking from one machine to another. Some people could come home from the gym with an added 500 calories to deal with, requiring high impact aerobics to burn it off.

Joining a gym leads people to believe they are losing weight when, in fact, it's getting worse in many cases. It's a bit like saying we have become religious so now have an excuse to still be a bad person. We are fooling ourselves.

Of course, that's an extreme example, and many of us know how many calories are in wine and beer and how to work them off. But what isn't considered is that many people in the food industry are happy that we don't know how much hidden sugar and fat we and especially our children consume every day, so knowledge should be your new "diet." Always start with knowledge before you approach any problem, or you'll fail.

That is my approach to eating chocolate. I know exactly how long it takes to work off 1.6 ounces of candy. An easy way to estimate how many minutes of excerise would be required is to divide the calorie content by 10. That's low though, and you could easily burn off more; if you push harder it goes up to 15 calories a minute. So, for example, next time you have a 250-calorie chocolate bar, assume it will take around 25 minutes (divide by 10) on a rowing machine or another exercise to burn it off and 25 times less time to eat it. It's easy math. Some products like giant lollipops and Easter eggs, for example, can have over 800 calories; that's 1 hour and 20 minutes hard on a cross-trainer.

Or put it another way: with the average kid in the UK, and I am sure this is common in many countries, receiving 8.8 hollow chocolate Easter eggs over the Easter break, it's not surprising we have a problem. It's not your fault or the kid's fault that the eggs are so appealing; Easter eggs in 2016 were reported to be on sale in Tesco and Sainsbury's supermarkets as early as January, so even if you resist for a while, you may eventually give in if you are regularly tempted by them. Some chocolate Easter eggs on sale in the UK have about 1,600 calories, if we suvive that, it's then Valentine's day, Halloween, and Christmas. Yes, all highly profitable occasions that are seen by producers as opportunities to sell us more sweets.

If people didn't eat Easter eggs, say for just one year, we would save $653 million—and that's enough cash to build a brand-new hospital in the UK.

When I was on the rowing machine, I would put my headphones on, get into a rhythm, and row for 6.2 miles. I don't know if any of you readers are rowers, but at fifty-one years old I did that 10 k, often with my amazing son Leon, in just over 39 minutes and 25 seconds, and that gobbled up at least 600 calories in one hit. My scores put me in the top ten people in my age group in the world indoor-rowing rankings. I would be dripping sweat and utterly exhausted after the races, and for what? Roughly the same calories as a Big Mac. Imagine that pain in the gym before you eat it.

In essence, I have managed to row off the candy, but as a result I have worn my knees out. Six operations to both knees have been a very heavy price to pay. I have covered tens of thousands of miles on Concept2 rowing machines, but I wore my meniscus knee cartilages out doing so, and nowadays I sometimes find it hard to take the kids to the shopping mall without my left knee giving me trouble. I might see my anesthetist with the funny eyebrows one last time. It turns out that the original knee operation may have missed a bit of torn cartilage, causing the current pain, and also opened up a channel where the synovial fluid leaks into the back of my knee and calf. Plus, I am getting older and things that used to heal up in weeks twenty years ago now take months. I have a beastly thing called a "bursar" on the back of my joint, but I think it will go away in the end. It's all because I'm a man who loves chocolate.

As you can imagine, rowing and being a chocolate eater used to be neatly compatible, but now I *really* have to think first about what I eat. You can't win. That is why, after all that, I had to look so hard into how much sugar I was eating, from where, and how long it would take to burn it off. I can still swim, walk, write, and think. I work out with very light rowing, too, and have cut a lot of hard alcohol and wine out of my diet. I have also tried to stop snacking and cut a considerable number of sweet foods from what I eat. I hope it makes you feel a little better to hear that I struggle too, like everyone else, in the battle against putting on weight in the face of a sugar-loaded food industry.

It's not just the calories, there is another potential hazard—my teeth. I had them all capped at great expense for the job at hand. I had my middle teeth capped many years ago, when they were still okay, then, later, after chatting with my good London dentist, we thought it would be best to do all of them in advance, knowing how much candy was on the way in.

So that's how I keep my health the same—it works for me and answers one of the questions that I am asked the most.

––––––––––––

Now, before you think I take pleasure in seeing people of all ages gulping down sweets like frenzied pelicans, let's start by saying that it does trouble me. I represent an industry that potentially makes people overweight and can rot their teeth. Is this really a dream? I'm not overly proud of that fact. Nevertheless, I confess that chocolate is also the substance that boosted my profile in national and international newspapers, as well as on television, and made me an author. Furthermore, it kept me alive on many occasions in my youth. In fact, I don't think I would be alive if it were not for candy.

I carved my job out of nothing. The whole thing is ridiculous. I am said to be a real-life Willy Wonka, albeit irreversibly cynical after being a journalist for so long and listening to so much sales literature that people have wanted me to publish in my journals. Cynicism for me is a pleasurably incurable disease. And yes, they could replace the sugar in your chocolate bar with sugar replacements, remove a good chunk of the fat with emulsifiers, and use these new scientific breakthroughs to reduce the calories by as much as 40 percent. They do that already in France, Germany, and Spain, but not in the UK so much or in the US. Most, at least in Europe, seem to have made the product smaller for the same price.

However, chocolate does have an attraction. Like many sweets, it's a statement of self-indulgence, our moment in time. When I eat a chocolate and sink back into the couch (if the five kids and my knee let me) and I offer one to my wife, I am doing what makes Angus Kennedy more of who *he* wants to be, namely a man with free choice.

It's time to get things straight. I'm going to tell you a few things you probably never knew about the chocolate industry as well as the fact that we narrowly escaped running out of chocolate. Take where it comes from (originally), for example: nice, quaint little chocolate factories? Think again: most chocolate, in Europe especially, is made, that is *premade*, by just four companies that dominate the entire global industry. And by corporations that you may never have even heard of.

Also spare a thought for the products that you *don't* see on your shelves. It was reported by Statista in 2016 that Hershey had a 44 percent US market share, with Mars at 29 percent. Between them, their share of the US market is huge at 73 percent. If you add in Lindt/ Ghirardelli and Nestlé's share, my guess is that this leaves around 12 percent of the shelves available for all other global chocolate producers and artisans, of which there are tens of thousands. It doesn't leave much room, in my opinion, to enjoy some of the truly unique chocolate brands that I have tasted over thirty years.

So what are the factories actually like? Let's take you on a magical journey right into the units I have been to, and then we can move on to find out if, as there have been rumors, we really will run out of chocolate.

CHAPTER 13

What You Might Not Know
About Your Chocolate Bar

It's said that the very first sweet was made out of honey, as sugar wasn't discovered until much later, and it's safe to say that it was combined with fruits from the ancient Indians and Chinese. Sugar was known in Roman times, but they used it mainly for medicine.

Confectionery is a relatively recent invention. In the Middle Ages, "sweetmeats" were only for the very wealthy, and they took the form of products such as gingerbread, sugared almonds, and marzipan. As sugar became cheaper during the nineteenth century, boiled sweets were developed and given the name *candy*, which comes from Sanskrit *kahnda*, which literally means *piece of sugar*.

Modern marshmallows were invented around 1850 and fudge, it's thought was first made in the US in the 1880s, so most of the products we see nowadays are relatively modern compared to other favorites, such as wine. In Victorian times, many candies were cooked in pots and molded by hand on marble tables. It was in the early 1900s that more sophisticated chocolate molding and tempering machines started to appear, and candy cookers could make far bigger batches, changing things forever.

Today some of these factories are producing hundreds of tons a day. I went to see a modern chocolate molding and cooling line last week in Denmark that was over 260 feet long and 31 inches wide, capable of producing three tons of chocolate an hour. And it was a small one. They go up to the length of a 328-foot-long Olympic running track, three feet wide and producing up to ten tons an hour. On top of this, some chocolate factories could easily have up to ten of these huge lines in one factory side by side, so production is vast, up to one hundred tons an hour. That's equivalent to thirty-three of my Toyota Land Cruiser 4 x 4s in weight in chocolate every single hour of the day. And running twenty-four hours a day, too, nonstop. It is truly staggering to see how much chocolate we all eat.

———

Today, you might think that it's just cocoa powder, fats, milk, sugar, and a few other bits and pieces in your favorite chocolate bar. Think again. You've got trees in some of your chocolate bars. Well, a lot of your chocolate bars, as chocolate is a by-product of trees—but we're not just talking about cocoa trees.

Recently I visited a gigantic biochemical plant in Norway that uses a by-product of the spruce tree to make something called "vanillin" (a vanilla replacer). That's right, you may even have some spruce tree extracts in your chocolate bar.

The most expensive ingredients in chocolate are things such as vanilla, cocoa powder, and cocoa butter. Therefore, if producers can invent something less expensive that tastes just like vanilla and replace it, that's a bit more profit. And no one really notices that much, either, because vanillin is a clever ingredient.

As I said before, they can't take all the cocoa butter out of chocolate, as it would no longer technically be chocolate and they would have to call it "vegelate." Doesn't sound so nice, right? They can, however, *not state* the percentage of cocoa butter on the packet (which I believe more producers should). The more they use, the better in general the quality of your chocolate bar. Many producers, nonetheless, will mix it with cheaper vegetable fat, so it could be 90 percent fat and just 10 percent cocoa butter. But it's still chocolate (just). More reputable producers state their cocoa butter content on the packet, which is a noble thing to do.

High-quality chocolate will have a high percentage of cocoa butter and generally less sugar (sugar and vegetable fat are cheap). Cocoa butter and cocoa powder, which when combined are called "cocoa liquor," are very expensive. The way to test a quality chocolate bar is to snap it in half or break a segment off. A cheap product with very low cocoa butter content will not make a nice click or a snapping noise when you break off a piece. Instead, it will bend and make a soft sound, with hardly a snapping noise at all. Also, if you close your eyes and pop some chocolate into your mouth, some has so much sugar it doesn't even taste like chocolate anymore. That makes it a cheap and low-end product.

The fact that I had to adhere to a secrecy agreement before visiting the Norway vanillin plant boosted my inquisitiveness. You see, I don't just visit the chocolate factories. I also pay regular trips to the ingredients companies that make flavors and specialist ingredients such as oils, emulsifiers, milk powders, colors, and sweeteners, for example. That's not including the ingenious processing and packaging machinery suppliers that provide the industry with super high-tech machines, some so big they leave the factory gates the sizes of my kids' bedrooms.

One machine I saw in Italy last month was a cocoa press, a machine designed to press the cocoa butter out of the cocoa powder. When you are up close to a brand-new one of these, with your palm resting on its cold steel surface, as it stands shining in the warehouse ready to go to Peru or somewhere deep into South America, it has a real presence. Some hydraulic cocoa presses are longer than a house and weigh in at eighteen tons and have more power than dozens of Ferraris. It's an amazing piece of engineering when you get up close, and almost a work of art.

This is just one of hundreds of different types of machines that are carefully crafted and exported each year around the globe, and they come complete with whole new impossible-to-newcomers vocabulary, including *conches, tempering units, servo-assisted robotics, depositors, vertical form fill seal-packing units, bunch wrappers, molding lines, five-roll refiners, cartoners, egg spinners, extruders, flow wrappers, bucket elevators,* and even *vibrators.*

Modern factories have very few people wandering around. These machines are so efficient that you might just about spot the odd person in a white coat, a hairnet, and white wellies or black factory-issue shoes popping in and out from a see-through plastic swinging door, looking satisfied, ticking a box on a clip chart, and then disappearing again.

You also don't see much moving product in a modern chocolate factory anymore, as most units now tend to be sealed with casings, with small windows to look in, so we don't potentially insert our arms and have an accident. There is often a control room, normally a little higher up on the floor level, which looks more like a giant airplane cockpit with screens everywhere telling everything about the production. Though modern machines now are so intelligent they show you videos of what they are doing and can do, and are really quite clever.

Of course, not all factories have this much investment or are that high-tech, but if you were thinking of starting a high-tech chocolate production line, you would be talking about an investment in the tens of millions of dollars. A single chocolate molding line, say a two-hundred-foot line capable of producing five tons an hour, will set you back something in the region of $4 to $5 million. That's just the molding machine—the one that molds your chocolate into shape. On top of that you will need a factory, flooring, tempering machines, cooling tunnels, packing machines, conveyors, shrink wrappers, wall-mounted bug killers, clothing, metal detectors, packing materials, ingredients. It's endless.

I have been to the largest chocolate factory in the world, which is in Belgium, and I know I am approaching, even with my eyes closed, at around a mile away. If I open the windows of the car I can smell the wonderful chocolate. Must be a cool place to live. Yes, you really can smell the big chocolate factories when you get near one.

The larger factories are complete with vast halls full of humming machines, some very noisy, and it's often quite hot, especially near the bean roasters, but everywhere you go there is an amazing aroma of chocolate emanating from their depths. However, as you can imagine, factories are only as efficient as the machines that are installed. New machines and technologies tend to come out every three years, and these new innovations are announced at the giant trade shows (in Germany). There is another show (Interpack) that covers sixty-four acres and is filled with twenty giant halls full of machines the size of buses. You need a bicycle to get from one machine to the next.

I would say most factories I have visited combine old and new machines and keep updating. Some factories still run on forty- to fifty-year-old (often adapted) machines that keep going year after year. I often come across manufacturers who buy the machines and adapt them themselves, but it's always top secret and I am whisked past them quickly, before I can take a photo.

So big is the Interpack trade exhibition in Germany that sells all these machines, that it's not really an exhibition; it's more of a trade town, pretty much the size of an Olympic village. It's not a single hall, but many buildings, like giant warehouses packed with machines in halls the size of aircraft hangers, covering what seems to be endless square kilometers of plant and equipment. You have to get a bus or cycle from one end to the other. You might be able to walk, but you wouldn't have much time left to see the machines. It's rather curious to see men in business suits racing around the show on mini scooters, but there is no efficient way they could get around without them.

It's massive, truly massive, but fitting: the global confectionery industry is worth just under $150 billion per annum, and that's not including cakes and other sweet foods. The machines are what enable the shapes, tastes, and textures of your products to exist. Some of the most amazing ones are the enrobers, pieces of kit that will cover anything in chocolate, even a person (though it's not advisable). An enrober is basically a giant curtain of liquid chocolate that the product (a biscuit or marshmallow, for example) goes through and comes out covered neatly in chocolate. Some people's dream, I guess.

Chocolate tanks are pretty cool, too. These are giant and sometimes open-topped pots with hundreds of metric tons of liquid milk chocolate swirling around, which can make you feel dizzy. While filming for a program in New York, I almost had to catch a TV presenter when she leaned in a bit too far, right over this huge vat of swirling liquid chocolate, in a daze. The modern ones are closed. She just kept peering over the edge, going farther and farther, as if she were following a kind of mystical god from the ancient scriptures. She started to lean so far into the pot that I thought she was going to fall, so I grabbed her shoulder and pulled her back. She woke up with a start and later admitted she was entranced looking into the seductive and mesmerizing swirls of chocolate.

Recently, near Moscow, a lady who was working in a factory, dropped her phone in a chocolate mixing tank. I think it was a very old mixing tank, as this should not happen now. She wanted her phone back so tried to reach down into the swirling mixing tank to get it. Unfortunately, she fell in and was most likely mangled up before drowning in chocolate. That's a shocking way to go. The mixing arms would have pulled her down and literally pulped her with the chocolate. Ouch. I have visited a lot of factories in Russia. Many are super high-tech, but the kit they use is often very old, so they can result in tragedy.

I like the almost humanlike robots (pick-and-place machines) that pick a chocolate product off a conveyor belt. With their little air suction hands, they recognize the chocolate bunny they want, take it off the conveyor belt, and place it beautifully in a chocolate assortment with other different shapes and sizes. It's amazing to watch. It's like they're capable of thinking. I just want to go up to one, start chatting, and say to it, in midaction, "Hey, you missed one chocolate over there, mate." I bet it would stop, take a look around, locate me, look me in the eye, and then tell me, "No, I didn't."

Then there are the high-tech machines that pack, twist, and wrap candies at a speed of two thousand individual candies a minute. They are some of the fastest packing machines in the world. It's a blur. You can't actually see them working because they go so fast, and still they get faster, better, and more economical, reliable, durable, safer, brighter, and lighter—it never stops, every year they're better and better. One of the factories that make some of these majestic machines gives its creations names like "Anna" or "Christina" while assembling them on the factory floor. The engineer writes the name on the side of the machine in pencil on sticky tape. It's almost as if they are producing people, they care so much for them.

I recently went to a Polish raspberry processing plant in the middle of nowhere. It was a nine-hour drive in an old Volkswagen Golf across the country. I arrived in a place where they make raspberry puree (an ingredient for cakes and chocolates) in this huge factory near the Ukrainian border. I have never seen so many raspberries growing in one place, as they showed me the farms too. Seriously, it was the biggest field I have ever seen. We were taken along part of a line of raspberry canes that ran for over forty miles. I thought that a line of six feet in my nasty, polluted garden in the UK where I tried and failed to grow them was good. They are all picked by hand, too.

This Polish raspberry puree factory has three miles of pipes. That means it's around a one-hour walk to see them all. And that was just the piping, nothing compared to other things, I am told. Many of my customers that travel say they have seen fields in Russia that are so big it takes six hours to drive from one end to the other.

Some chocolate factories are truly magnificent and almost run themselves. China, India, Nigeria, South Africa, Russia, Turkey, and even Vietnam are all now classified as having huge market potential with an up to 213 percent increase in consumption, so we need them. I see so much money being made and always think, *Angus, you so need to get your act into gear and make chocolates.*

I have seen a lot of smaller chocolate producers that handmake their confectionery, as well as medium-sized companies that have a mix of modern and older production tools. I have also spent some time working on the packaging line in a factory in the UK. A lot of products are still packed by hand, as machines can cost well over $500,000 each.

Chocolate makers are really amazing people. I mean, these wonderful ladies with huge forearms (they tend to be women) are there together on the line and facing one another, one on each side of the conveyor, laughing and joking all the time and full of spirit. Still happy, after having been packing chocolates into cartons nearly all their lives. These people for me are often the ones I remember the most.

You never know what's around the corner. Some self-styled chefs and "artists," as they prefer to be called, are getting amazing money for artisan handmade chocolates. In Brussels, for instance, I went to a chocolate tasting session and it was arranged so that I could walk into any chocolate shop on an exclusive street, where all the chocolate boutiques are located, and eat anything I wanted. It was a sponsored tour, and of course I walked into nearly all the chocolate boutiques and tried everything!

Some boutiques were so exclusive they were called *galleries* and you could not even find "the chocolate" for sale in them. I went inside one that was dark and laid out like an art gallery. I would eventually find "the chocolate" with a single LED spotlight on it, sitting on some giant bronze sculpture. Each chocolate cost up to seventeen dollars, so a small box of nine chocolates would be up to $160.

I came out of the shop holding a small box of chocolates that cost over one hundred dollars, and passed a homeless man who couldn't even afford a hot drink and a bag of chips. That's wrong to me, but that's normal life for others.

Factories are changing fast. I still remember how many people I used to see working on the lines in factories thirty years ago as I went around with my mother—hundreds of people handpacking and singing as they worked. It's a shame that there are factories that have lost that human touch. Machines are advertised with their *payback* time in labor costs and energy saved, so you get your money back as you cut wages. It's a human cost. The machines always win, and many investors get their money back on the investment in a machine in less than two years. Unfortunately, the staff are laid off, which is sad but inevitable.

The big guys get bigger to reflect new global demand. A chocolate factory nowadays will have a line of machines to make your average molded chocolate wafer product, and each machine will produce a wafer sheet more than three hundred feet long. Now imagine there are many of these lines, row after row. You can enter the factory and find endless rows of three-hundred-feet-long machine lines, literally miles in total length, and you can hear the humming, clicking, and hissing of thousands of tons of chocolate product being made, every single day, every hour, hundreds of thousands of tons leaving for places all over the world.

Of course, these machines cost millions of dollars, and I have been to visit just about every company that makes them. They are all run by my friends who are always coming up with something new. As it is such a huge investment to start a large chocolate factory, the big guys just get bigger and bigger and gobble up anything and anyone that competes with them.

It's often more amazing to visit the suppliers to the chocolate producers, as they are the pulse of the industry, mainly because your chocolate bar is often limited by the technology employed to produce it.

My Norway trip was a memorable occasion and a great example of what it's like to see these places. I was sent to find out all about vanillin. I was met at the airport and taken to a location to stay the night before the next day's factory site trip. It's normally a hotel, but in this case, I was given the keys to an entire beach house next to the sea.

I had the whole house to myself, with wine in the fridge, food, and a "Welcome Angus" packet, along with more chocolate placed in thoughtful places. *Wow, good start*, I thought. When I went to compliment my hosts on the accommodations, they were happy to inform me that they owned not just the beach house I stayed in, but also most of the beach houses along the whole stretch of beach. In fact, they owned the whole beach as well. Upon further questioning, it became clear that they also owned much of the peninsula.

I was taken to a giant site, a few miles of square land that contained thirteen factories, each the size of a normal factory. And here is where I saw, for the first time, giant spruce trees being ground up in spectacularly large machines that turn a huge tree into pulp right in front of you in seconds. It's terrifying standing in front of this tree crusher. All I could think of while I was standing next to this monster machine was, *You definitely don't want to fall into that one, Angus.*

The trees are then made into bioproducts for the food industry, I was told. As I walked around the plant, the labs, vast areas of land, trees, and impossibly intelligent people wearing cool Joe 90–type glasses everywhere made me feel like I was walking through a modern scene from the science fiction film *The Day of the Triffids.*

The factory came complete with its own hydroelectric plant and river dam, thousands of square miles of land, old Victorian paper mills, private castles, and collections of art that I was taken to see if I promised I would not say *what* I had seen. It was truly astonishing.

And all this is so that chocolate producers don't have to buy expensive vanilla. It's safe to say that you never know what you are going to see, and you always think you are prepared when in fact you aren't. But this place exists for a small word on your chocolate bar, *vanillin*—it's in a lot of chocolate. On the plus side, the company always plants more trees than they process. Norway is a wonderful country, and its people are amazing and I would go back tomorrow if I had the slightest excuse. I was told by my hosts that they don't have road rage, arguments, or much stress. Was this country a hidden heaven? Or were they joking with me? Being a stressed-out, argumentative Brit, I was ready to argue with them, to which they didn't argue, which of course they thought was very funny. You can't win.

No one trip is the same, though.

I had an unusual experience when I was invited to Moscow to visit a Russian machinery factory that supplied bakery depositors, a kind of machine that injects jam into a donut, I normally get picked up by a taxi or find my way on public transport, but this time I was collected by not one but three blacked-out Škodas. I was to travel in the middle car. There was one car at the front and one at the back, inches behind me and with only a foot or so to spare between all three of them as we sped away from the airport at high speed. Perhaps they thought I was some kind of CIA agent and had picked up the wrong man. Perhaps I would never be seen again. For an Englishman in Kent who never sees much snow, to be driven at high speed along snow-covered streets is another experience altogether. I did eventually arrive at the factory, where my host, an eccentric and likable young Russian man with a lot of money (I didn't ask where it came from) was keen to show me his wealth.

We saw the factory, and in my opinion, it was one that unfortunately demonstrated how not to manage people. It was a kind of "if they don't like it, they are out" type of set up. And after seeing a few dejected employees, I was taken away, but this time for lunch in a very fast car. It looked like some kind of Formula Two car. The driver's foot hit the pedal, my head pressed into the headrest, and I was relieved to get back to the hotel. Well, temporarily.

Back at the hotel, another curiosity presented itself. I found myself in a hotel with "extra services." Not long after I checked in, my room phone rang and a person on the other end asked me directly if I wanted "extras." They seemed to know my name, too, which was a little off-putting.

"Hey, Mr. Kennedy, you want something extra tonight? We come now, your room, no problem."

Being curious, I opened the door of my hotel room to take a look, and the whole corridor was full of women hanging out and not wearing much at all, checking me out immediately as I peered out. I slammed the door in a cold sweat, fell back against it, and then retired back to my room. The phone rang again.

"Why not, Mr. Kennedy? We do good rate."

I kept to my morals and needless to say I didn't sleep much at all wondering what on earth was being done in the rooms on my floor.

Morning finally dawned and I put on my suit and checked out and didn't say a word about it. My host arrived with two crash helmets in his arms, perhaps I needed more impressing. I was being picked up on a snow bike. I had never even seen one before. It seemed to be a cross between a powerful motorbike and snowmobile that could go spectacularly fast on snow and ice. And all I had to keep me warm and protected was an inadequate blue suit and tie from Marks and Spencer, hardly made for the job of careering through Moscow on the back of a snow bike.

My host took a detour, and it wasn't long before he zoomed off toward a frozen lake with his Englishman cargo clinging on desperately. When we hit the open ice, he squeezed the throttle open and we must have hit 120 miles an hour. All I had was my tie (now blown backward and frozen rigidly), along with a thin cotton jacket, matching trousers, and a shirt. I survived, obviously, but you never know what might be in store. I must say, though, it was impressive, even if everything else was questionable.

Still, the industry keeps coming up trumps with surprise after surprise, especially when it comes to the properties of the product. It's full of tried-and-tested marketing garbage, but then so are most industries. The amount of money that gets pumped into researching the benefits of chocolate is vast, so let's check out all the things it could do. Why eat anything else?

Just some of the claims I have come across regarding the properties of chocolate are as follows: it can improve brain performance, help you relax, improve sex, help with insulin sensitivity, reduce stress in expectant mothers, improve your hair, prevent sunburn, and enhance moods. You name it, chocolate can do it, so roll up, roll up, and look no further than your cupboard for cures, all with a single product. There is no point in eating anything else, because chocolate can do it. I like the way they tend to use the words "can" and "may help to," to make their ever more outlandish chocolate-can-do claims arguably true.

It has even been reported to "potentially" help you lose weight. Chocolate is also reported to be the second-most-fattening food product in the world, so I am not sure how they came up with the losing weight claim.

I read a report recently that said chocolate can even be good for brain injuries such as concussions. Okay, as if I'm really going to march out of the accident unit of the Maidstone General Hospital and demand a Galaxy bar, though it's a pleasurable thought to have one. As you read earlier, I had a huge blow to my head, and it was breathing into a paper bag that chocolate may have been in, not actual chocolate, that saved me.

With all the money they put into research, and it's significant, they are probably going to say that chocolate is great for the prevention of alien abduction the next time you go for a picnic down the Topanga Canyon in California. Yes, you don't need anything other than chocolate.

Oh yes, they claim it all. They have made us believe, and successfully, that chocolate can be healthy. But then to do that, you only need to find *one* tiny thing that is healthy about it and *only* talk about that.

You cannot blame them. We are in a world that consumes over 7.3 million metric tons a year. All this is not bad, considering that the first chocolate bar was molded by Fry's in the UK in 1847, which isn't that long ago.

As a nation, though the US consumes the most total chocolate, Americans are actually fairly conservative chocolate eaters and only eat twelve pounds per head per year. That's far less than the amount consumed by the gluttonous English, who shovel down a whopping 26.5 pounds per head per year. Basically, it's a race between the UK, Ireland, Switzerland, and Germany to top the eating per capita records. Is it a good thing to be on top of the league table of gluttony? I leave that up to you to decide.

One thing I do know is that we are eating more chocolate than ever, with the average man in the UK said to be eating six chocolate bars a week, more than the average woman. Women are proven to think about it more, though, on average three times a day.

The world is going wild for chocolate, there is no escaping that fact, but come on, we don't buy chocolate for its health benefits, do we? Who are they kidding? Personally, I don't eat chocolate to be healthy; I stay healthy so I can eat chocolate.

It's not very difficult to work out why people crave it so often. It contains caffeine (addictive), sugar (claimed to be addictive), and theobromine, a natural relaxant, so you can feel relaxed, alert, and addicted all at the same time. Job done, game, set, and match. The desire is not necessarily derived from a love for the product, in my opinion it's likely a love for the chemicals to which one is addicted.

Perhaps I am being a bit harsh, but can't we just eat something and enjoy it without the spin? And enjoy it we must, as there are rumors that the world could run out of chocolate. Yours truly was actually the one who made this headline by mentioning it to the press a few years ago, in 2012. So are we really going to run out of chocolate? Well, in some ways we already have.

CHAPTER 14

Will We Run Out of Chocolate?

Mirror, mirror, on the wall, will our
chocolate NOT run out after all?

Now, *there* is a question. It's widely known that chocolate consumption ebbs and flows. And since I started writing this book, it's all changed.

Again.

Nothing ever stays the same with chocolate anyway, as the industry moves on so fast.

It's a haunting question that so many people have been asking: could we run out of chocolate? Admittedly, fewer people are asking this now. However, the big issue for us all is, will we eat less chocolate and less sugar in general? I believe so. The process has already started, and it will continue for many years. The landscape of what confectionery we eat will be very different within the next ten years.

It's no longer so much a question of whether we will run out of chocolate. It is more, will our grandchildren believe us when we tell them that our chocolate bars used to be so much bigger and sugary than they are now, and eaten with the knowledge of how unfair, in my opinion, it's farmed and how our planet and children may have suffered in the process?

Firstly then, is there going to be a cocoa and chocolate shortage? The answer is, no. However, what caused the threat deserves attention. Was it media frenzy or reality?

It was actually a bit of both. There was a threat of a shortage, and in many ways there still is, but a different type of shortage. In fact, there is a more sinister threat to the entire industry if it doesn't come to grips with some major issues right now.

Media stories tend to have at least an element of truth to them. They were right to report that we *could* have run out of chocolate, so brace yourselves for how that happened. They could equally say that we *could* see the arrival of a new, massive life-changing planet creeping into our solar system—and that would certainly wipe out chocolate. Anything *could* happen.

All media companies want to attract a wider audience, and fear-based stories such as "Hey Folks, We're All Going to Die Tomorrow in a Nuclear War" and "Freak Snowstorms Are Coming to Kill Us"—which never seem to happen—tend to make us worry and subsequently buy into fearmongering media.

The potential chocolate shortage was recognized before 2012 by one or two experts, and it was generally accepted knowledge that a problem was looming. Then in 2012, a lecture at the London Chocolate Forum mentioned that we *could* run out of chocolate in eight years' time—2020—right in front of the press.

The journalists landed the dream story that they were looking for and went on to make it a huge story. The takeaway was generally that we *could* run out of chocolate, not necessarily that we *will* run out (depending on your chosen media outlet). It's been in the media ever since and continues to get attention.

So, what's the problem? Well, it started with the cocoa bean. The cocoa bean is to chocolate what the grape is to wine: it produces cocoa powder and cocoa butter, which are used in chocolate production.

It was said at that time of the predicted shortage that production of cocoa had dropped, and the trend was predicted to grow. Demand had outstripped production. But experts thought the trend would continue, and it didn't. It appears that it's stabilized, so there won't be a cocoa or a chocolate shortage. If anything, we may have too much cocoa. But I believe, more interestingly, that in the future we will have far less trusting consumers and that more people will be scrutinizing their processed food, looking for higher quality organic products with fewer additives and less sugar.

In recent years chocolate consumption actually shrunk, and the trend is set to continue in mature markets.

No one understood the full impact of the antisugar drive and the threat of taxes on consumption, which like most taxes seem inevitable. The government allowed us to consume as much sugar as possible in the UK for as long as we wanted it. Sugar consumption was left to rise beyond healthy limits, and consumption was almost ignored as everyone focused on the fat content while ignoring sugar. Sugar was even added to our diets without us knowing. Now that we are all hooked on it (I believe it can be addictive), they plan tax it.

Cocoa and chocolate have also become very fashionable products and in hot demand, which fueled the running out story. Cocoa powder is stuffed into everything from your morning cappuccino to a tin pot of lip balm. I recently spotted Japanese chocolate cheese slices and chocolate covered bacon and cocoa self-tanning wipes.

Can't we just eat it?

The increased demand for cocoa now comes from many industries, not just the chocolate inudstry. This fueled the scare.

But could we have missed the issue entirely? I would say the cocoa production industry is in a spot of trouble. I read recently that, out of many, if not all, of the commercial crops grown—from wheat to corn to barley—cocoa, up until recently, was the *only* crop that hadn't increased its yield since 1930. This is due mainly to a lack of investment in the past. The industry is trying hard now to change this. However, many of the other arable crops have seen around a tenfold increase per hectare, while cocoa up until recently has seen almost zero. It's a case of a little bit too little too late, I believe.

What's wrong with cocoa farming, why is it in such a state? A lot is wrong, is the answer to that.

First, cocoa beans aren't easy to grow. Cocoa trees can easily become infected by diseases. In fact, every year, according to the Food and Agriculture arm of the United Nations, up to 40 percent of all cocoa production is wiped out by disease and fungi. The crops can be attacked by lurgies with horrible names such as frosty pod rot, cacao swollen-shoot virus, and a particularly vindictive sounding vascular streak dieback. Some of these diseases can wipe out an entire crop. And we are talking about West African farmers with little money to solve it all, and some who are clearly having a bad time providing us with our good times with chocolate. You need money for insecticides.

The Ivory Coast produces the largest amount of cocoa in the world—up to 1.7 million tons annually, accounting for around 35 percent of our supply. Ghana produces the second largest amount, around 850,000 tons (depending on the year), but a lot of Ghanaian cocoa is smuggled through the border to the Ivory Coast, where, it's claimed, it can be sold for a better price than in Ghana.

To add to the dilemma, you can't just plant a tree and produce cocoa straightaway, as the new tree won't bear fruit for six years—unless it's a hybrid. Some are claiming that the taste of the hybrid is not up to standard compared to traditional, natural cocoa trees.

The Fairtrade Foundation says there are reported to be six million cocoa farmers—that is, families—around the world, many with very little money, whose farms are quite inaccessible as they are right in the depth of tropical jungles, with difficult terrain and dirt tracks winding up into the hills. You can see the uphill (literally) struggle they face. Some of these farms are so remote and so out of reach that the farmers have never actually eaten chocolate. It's claimed many don't know what it is, yet they spend their entire lives growing cocoa for us.

I have been told by many of my customers that you can offer some cocoa farmers (not just in the Ivory Coast) a bar of chocolate and they will eat the wrapper, too, as they have not seen a bar of chocolate before. I guess that's no different from showing Western chocolate consumers an open cocoa pod. They tend to have no idea what it is, and say it looks disgusting. Yes, disgusting—their favorite tasting product!

Other problems crop up for them: lack of rainfall; adverse climate; war and unrest; or simply that cocoa is too cheap, as it is at the moment, so people plant rubber trees instead or mine for gold in favor of farming cocoa trees.

Illegal mining in West Africa is horrific. These operations are said to spread mercury over the land, pretty much killing everything in its path, so nothing can be grown for years after it. I have met people who have seen it. Many large cocoa farms have been lost this way.

Cocoa farmers who do stick with it often don't have the knowledge required to prune their trees properly, money to plant new trees, and access to fertilizers. A large proportion of the trees are already very old, too old to produce a decent crop.

A lot of programs have been launched by the industry, investing millions of dollars to help and educate cocoa farmers and provide training, but there's still a long way to go. Many reporters claim there has been little progress, especially when it comes to child labor. On top of all that, some famers have to negotiate with their own governments—and that is quite a task as they can only sell their beans at a set price to the government agencies.

Eventually we *may* need more cocoa if we really are going to have to feed as many as nine billion people by 2050, but farmers already have a massive job on their hands just surviving.

So, there are many reasons that chocolate makes me a sad person working in what's perceived to be one of the happiest industries.

Chocolate faces two formidable opponents right now that I believe will affect its long-term future. The first is health: chocolate is around 50 percent sugar, and the other half is fat. Secondly, people are gradually becoming aware of young children working on the farms and how the farmers are struggling and living below the poverty line, and that will, in my opinion, continue to affect sales. It doesn't take long for things to lose favor, especially when it comes to consumers who also have children, demanding transparency and explanation.

The organization Slave Free Chocolate reports that there are approximately 1.8 million children in the Ivory Coast and Ghana who may be exposed to the worst forms of child labor on cocoa farms. This is an extremely sensitive issue for all of us, including the governments who are, I believe, also trying hard to stop it. When I inquire about child labor in my profession, and I know some very senior people, I'm often met with an awkward reluctance to speak openly. Of course I am, people could lose their jobs and shareholders tend not to like bad stories. I understand this. People have to make money, but, still, the industry wants to see improvement and people are frustrated that it's not moving fast enough. No one in the industry wants this to continue.

Many of the children who work in the cocoa industry are not even paid. Admittedly, some farmers' children are helping their parents, and many parents send their children to work on the neighboring farms. My kids empty the dishwasher (if I am lucky) and do things at home like giving their younger siblings baths or helping me plant the vegetable patch. But this, sadly, is more sinister.

The website End Slavery Now claims that there are children, some as young as five, who have been (and still are) kidnapped from small villages to work in the farms. It's claimed they are taken against their will from small villages in neighboring African countries, such as Burkina Faso and Mali, two of the poorest countries in the world.

In the film *The Dark Side of Chocolate* directed by Miki Mistrati, Miki reports that children are being taken by traffickers on mopeds across the border to work on farms. It's not an easy film to watch. I believe it's true and I have spoken with him in person about his experiences. Sometimes the parents sold their kids into slavery without knowing what the implications were.

Children are reported to start work at six in the morning and work until dusk, often using chainsaws, machetes, and heavy tools. The beans are packed into sacks that can weigh up to 100 pounds when full, and children are said to be beaten if they don't carry them. Farmers often provide kids with cheap food, including corn paste and bananas, and they can be given just a few planks to sleep on with meager sanitary conditions. Cases have been reported of children being whipped for working slowly or trying to escape.

Of course, not all chocolate is produced through child labor, far from it, and not all farmers are in such turmoil. There are many other cocoa growing regions and districts in the Ivory Coast, as well as around the world, without these problems.

The industry is trying very hard to end it, but it's a slow process. Many savvy chocolate producers in the UK, Switzerland, Germany, and other places are now buying land, growing their own cocoa, and managing their own farms, presumably treating their farmers well and producing excellent single-source chocolate (from one accountable farm). Their farms are being bought in Nicaragua, Ghana, Saint Lucia, and Cameroon, to name a few places.

Some are even sharing the profits with their farmers, which is in favor with consumers. This is a trend now and is set to continue as groups look to form and collectively buy land to manage their own farms, eradicate child labor and poverty issues, and subsequently build schools and essential infrastructures.

One cannot blame the entire industry or the governments. I know of countless ethical chocolate companies and organizations within the industry that are rightly appalled at what is going on and are trying hard to change things. Some retailers, too, are driving awareness and demanding transparency.

Many chocolate companies are involved in programs with governments to provide aid for schools, orphanages, water treatments, roads, and more. I know many people who personally go to see the farms for themselves and after are completely changed people. However, it's claimed that over 80 percent of the owners of chocolate companies have never been to a cocoa farm.

The industry is now providing consumers with a choice to buy according to their wishes, to eat a product not harvested by slaves, for example. I love chocolate hugely, but until this is over, chocolate will always have a slightly different taste for me. And may God help those kids.

The amount that farmers are given for their cocoa is another contentious issue. Actually, it's possibly the biggest issue, as if they had money, they then would have the investment to grow more cocoa, and it's arguable that they would not need so much cheap labor (kids) and have the incentive to continue farming.

According to the organization Make Chocolate Fair!, West African cocoa farmers, who are responsible for 70 percent of the world's cocoa production, earn on average just two dollars a day, perhaps even less; some reports claim just a dollar a day, especially now that the price of cocoa has plummeted. Women work extremely hard on the farms—it seems even harder than men—yet, I am told some earn up to 70 percent less than their male counterparts. Where's the incentive in that? It's a terrible wage anyway.

Look at it this way: if your dad is earning two dollars a day at sixty years old, surviving and scraping through every day of his life, you just won't want to do that job. You will want to go to a cool office if you can and not sweat in the depths of a jungle. No one can blame you. So, as you might imagine, parents are having a hard time persuading their kids to take over the family cocoa farm, which is another reason cocoa production is facing increasing challenges. In many areas, the next generation thinks being stuck on the farm is a lousy way to earn a living. And I thought it was tough persuading my kids to get into publishing!

Meanwhile, the industry aims in earnest to increase the yield for each farmer, so they have more volume to sell as opposed to them fighting for a better price. But it's not *always* the price per pound that is the problem.

Growing cocoa is a low-income job, and with fixed prices to sell the product to government agencies, I don't think it's fair. Most cocoa-growing countries have monopolistic cocoa associations that sell all the beans that are produced.

Some governments tend to set the price each year by taking into consideration the price achieved the previous year, forward contracts, and the harvest. But this can be unproductive due to the volatility of the price and exchange rates.

Some farmers have told me in person that they want free trade and to actually see the aid from the goodwill of the chocolate industry that apparently never seems to go their way. Poverty in West Africa cannot be solved by the chocolate industry alone. After millions in aid and numerous programs, many farmers are still not earning much more. I have met with farmers who claim they hadn't seen or heard of any aid.

In short, cocoa farming is a haven for problems of all shapes and sizes. There are a lot of issues to overcome as it is, so it's a difficult time for the industry. If things don't change soon and cocoa prices remain low, cocoa farmers may look for more lucrative crops, poten-tially to more slaves, or to abandon the farms completely, in which case demand *could* then exceed supply. The story has some great substance for debate. But in essence, farmers are the source of chocolate. The children are the source of its potential demise.

However a lot has been done to make a difference in the lives of those in cocoa farming, and we have made progress. But until now I feel the focus has traditionally been on the increased yield of the crop and not on the elimination of child labor.

Incidentally, there are many other regions, such as Ecuador, Peru, Bolivia, Cameroon, Dominican Republic, and Jamaica, and many others, that don't report such severe problems of child labor.

With all this in mind, I wouldn't become a cocoa farmer. Things have to change. One must be pretty desperate or completely inhu-mane to beat a child who doesn't carry a hundred pound bag of cocoa beans fast enough. That's not a farmer, that's a psychotic monster. I am sure there are many farmers who would not dream of doing such horrific things as buying children and subjecting them to cruelty or ill-treatment. Anyone who hurts, kidnaps, or violates a child's basic rights no matter how desparate they are needs psychiatric help.

If they are that evil, I can't see how we will change them in the short term. I reckon this type of farmer will keep using children and feeding them bananas to make more money. They are giving the indus-try a bad name; there are some wonderful people in farming.

How can you solve this and change an evil man into a good one? That's a very different type of aid altogether. Perhaps the chocolate industry has taken on too much and said it can solve what it can't. Only you and I, the consumers, can do that by being aware and forcing change.

In my opinion, the chocolate industry giants should have invested fifty years ago to help the six million farmers. That's improving now, though, and I know of ambitious projects set up to help. But still there are many skeptics.

One has to ask: could the industry have cheap cocoa without the farmers? Otherwise, where's the profit in the supply chains? This is a highly cynical summation, I know, but if the industry doesn't help them grow more, it can't make more chocolate and earn more profit. And shareholders won't invest in the industry unless it is seen to be doing something.

But let's be fair to the chocolate industry, too. It alone can't combat poverty in West Africa, and it has taken on a lot of promises—building roads, providing education knowledge funds, supplying fertilizers, trying to get kids into schools (that often need to be built). What about the *governments*? They are not to blame either, and they are the first to want to eradicate these sensitive issues. Throwing the blame makes a problem worse.

In the end, they say that if cocoa farmers were paid a sustainable price for their cocoa, one that better reflects how highly prized and loved chocolate is worldwide, they would stick with cocoa farming, not need to rely on children to work, and have the resources to invest in their farms. Only then might future generations consider it a viable occupation worth learning. And only then could I truly enjoy my bar of dark chocolate.

Anyway, I don't believe it's just the chocolate industry that should be under the spotlight. The whole processed food industry needs your attention. Now, after fifty years of reading about food, as I write, I am becoming a vegetarian. The food industry hides a lot of dark secrets.

In the meantime, how has your chocolate bar changed? It already has, and it will continue to do so. You may have noticed how different some chocolate tastes already compared to the chocolate of the 1980s. The type of bar you may eat in the future and how the chocolate will taste, and your opinion, too, may never be the same again.

CHAPTER 15

The Chocolate of the Future

When I close my eyes and taste a type of chocolate that I used to eat as a kid, I swear it's sweeter and less chocolaty now. There is no proof of this notion, of course, and many producers say they would never change their recipes. But I still feel, as do many consumers, that there have been recipe changes. Some chocolate doesn't actually taste like chocolate anymore. It just tastes plain sweet.

High prices of cocoa beans and sugar scares have had a big influence and changed a lot of products for good. Namely, the results are more expensive chocolate, different recipes—that is, chocolate made with less cocoa powder and cocoa butter—and smaller portions.

In all cases, you are likely to be buying less actual chocolate for the same price that you were in the early 2000s. Producers rightly claimed cocoa prices were too high, so we saw our products shrink. Well, now, the cocoa price has dropped, but will they make our bars bigger again? Doubtful. Nothing is ever that fair when people are making money.

If you're wealthy, you'll be okay. We still have the expensive stuff—chocolate with higher amounts of cocoa that reflects its rising price. The website bonappetit.com, for example, notes, "Lonohana's 70 percent cacao bar, made from just cacao and cane sugar, retails for $14. The full-cost of farmer operations is $25 per kilogram of cacao. High-quality cacao from other regions . . . goes for $7 to $9 per kilogram." Commodity cacao—what they claim you're getting in a standard chocolate bar—"is $3.50 per kilogram."

The vibrant and growing market for luxury and high-end chocolates is spreading rapidly across the globe. But you may also find that what used to be normal chocolate, for example a solid bar with 65 percent cocoa solids and at least 40 percent cocoa butter and no fillings, may now be a luxury product. Especially likely to become a luxury is single-source cocoa origin chocolate, i.e., a bar made from one, often small plantation. This is so the chocolate producer can trace all actions of the farmers and there is accountability for their well-being.

Technically it's not so much that we're running out of chocolate, but we're running out of what we can afford to buy and we already need to spend more to get the same amount of quality chocolate than we did just a few years ago. We're running out of grams of cocoa to the dollar. We won't run out of the cheaper, sugary, low-end products that are high in vegetable fat, low in cocoa butter, low in cocoa powder, and milkier.

Another way to make more profit out of a chocolate bar, considering cocoa is the most expensive ingredient, is to add things that aren't chocolate. So, welcome the new boys on the block: sugar (the cheapest), inclusions, vegetable fat, and air. The chocolate is simply no longer there in any great quantity. Bring on anything non-chocolate: fillings made with honey, mint extracts, fruits, air, nuts, sugar bases, glucose, nougats, caramels, marshmallows, and any other inclusion that could boost the weight and or size of the bar.

I have even heard of coloring a chocolate bar. It's possible, with the application of food coloring, to darken the color of a chocolate bar, making it look like it has a higher percentage of cocoa content than it does. I doubt that this is practiced often, and it might even be illegal, but it's entirely possible.

For mass-produced chocolate, your tastes and your attitudes might be gradually adapted to suit products with less cocoa, via new products and subtle changes to existing recipes. We might be getting used to a more sugary taste, too, without realizing it, to hide the fact there is less cocoa in the product. We might not appreciate it just yet, but some chocolate bars now don't snap like they used to, they just bend when you try to break them, a sure sign that they contain less cocoa butter. Perhaps that's another reason the giants are interested in new markets—consumers can be acclimated to the cheaper stuff with less cocoa powder and more sugar in the first place, and the company will see better profits.

Then again, as I mentioned previously, many producers would never change their recipe at all; in fact, most of them don't. But without changing the recipe and without raising the price, they're left with making their products smaller and thinner if they want to maintain a good profit margin, as the costs of many of their ingredients have been increasing.

They may make subtle changes to the shape, or there may be ingenious packaging designs to slow down our consumption speed or to give the appearance of the product being much larger than it is. Share packs, for example, with individually wrapped pieces of candy in a bag seem cute, but we are buying more packaging material, more air, and less chocolate.

A particularly clever example is the Toblerone bar, which managed to keep the same sized package that you see on the shelves, but when you unwrap it you find they have increased the gap between the triangles. Nonetheless, on the shelf it looks the same size: a brilliant move. Theodor Tobler, who invented this product in 1908, it's said, based the triangular segment design on Alpine scenery to create his chocolate mountain range–shaped bar.

I'm sorry, but to me, even though it tastes just as good, it now looks like the metal bicycle rack outside my local council library.

The rounded Dairy Milk chocolate bar, meanwhile, may look smooth and nice today, but just rounding its edges from its square shape took away 14 percent of its chocolate. It went from almost five ounces to a little more than four ounces for the same price. Again, nestled neatly within its wrapper, it looks like it's the same size as it used to be.

I actually think that a smaller confectionery product is a good thing, we don't need sugar in our diets. We eat enough already. We definitely don't need insanely large super-sized drinks (those should be banned!), so at least our chocolate bars are not getting bigger. But the price should drop when the size reduces and then it's fair.

I remember when I used to put a Mars bar in my pocket at school and it took up most of my pants. Today, I might have to take a second dig around to find it, as it's so much smaller. Okay, I have bigger pants and smaller hands, but still!

We might notice if they took an entire segment off our favorite bar. The bar would be shorter right away. Surely you can't sell that for the same price, right? I mean, if someone took out, say, 10 percent of my glass of wine and charged me the same price, I would rush back up to the bar and complain to the barman.

You'd think that in the same way, you can't just take a chunk off a bar of chocolate. But this is done.

It's sadly too common. And one of the winners has to be Quality Street, which, I read, in 1998 weighed in at a huge 3.7 pounds for a tin of assorted chocolates that could keep a family going for the whole of Christmas. Now it's less than half the size, just 1.7 pounds for a tub. That's about two pounds less of chocolate. That would now keep my kids going till Boxing Day at the very best.

The gold medal in bravery surely goes to Cadbury's, though, which reduced its six-pack of Cadbury Creme Eggs down to just a five-pack. Eggs traditionally come in half-dozens and dozens, don't they? Was that not the point of selling six in the first place? Taking the pack size down to five was a brilliant move on the face of it, but the media was furious about it and a lot of consumers were too. The move backfired somewhat, as it's claimed that angry consumers stopped buying the product, to the tune of, it's reported, an almost $8 million loss in sales after the change. But it's a profitable line now, I believe, so there was nothing we could do about it.

Producers don't want to change the taste of their product, understandably, so some just make it smaller—or in some cases promote it as having fewer calories.

It's a nice try, but *no*. It's not about fewer calories; you just sold me less chocolate for my buck. Let us have a cheaper price and be fair and I will decide if I need less chocolate, thanks. So there's no coincidence that many of your chocolate bars are smaller than they were five years ago.

In defense of the producers, they really had no choice then and many have not changed their product sizes. It's the *way* it was done by some producers that I feel was not correct. All of the sudden, your cherished chocolate bars were smaller but cost the same—I mean, almost a third of the size for some. Consumers should have been told about this shrinkage before the almost "secret change."

Producers across the food industry might have hoped they would get away with making their brands smaller without too much of a hoot, only to find that the newspaper journalists were of course having none of it. They noticed it all right, and tabloid journalists (many whom I know personally) were quick to notice. They are the best of any professionals at sniffing out something that isn't quite right. Never argue with a journalist. Pick anyone else, a politician preferably, because journalists don't let up.

Subsequently, they have slammed producers for tampering with product sizes or making any other adjustments. Some journalists I know keep products going back years, so they can tell the difference. They are brilliant at what they do.

These producers, I believe, honestly thought consumers might not notice that the product they had savored and loved for perhaps twenty years had suddenly shrunk to a miserable existence. But they forget that many consumers can count, have brains, do care, can see, can taste the difference, and do notice curious absences. They especially don't like to discover their product is smaller. This whole secret shrinking act is a slight insult to the intelligence of the consumer, who knows *damned well* if their product becomes smaller.

After all, many chocolate products are eaten with religious precision in the same way each time. Some consumers will suck products, nibble at them first, eat them whole, lick off the coconut, or break from the left corner first. However they do it, it is nearly always in the same unique, personal, and ceremonial way. Change the shape at your peril.

Ferrero told me last year that, according to their surveys, 94 percent of UK consumers *love* chocolate. And remember that they also told me that 90 percent of Americans vote chocolate as their favorite flavor. It's big. In my opinion, chocolate is not a matter of life and death; it's more important than that. It matters more relative to other products. If the price of baby wipes, let's say, went up, or if they were a centimeter shorter, many people would not bat an eyelid.

It's sad, but the same-price-for-less-product syndrome has taken its place in the history of chocolate. This is really nothing new within the entire food industry in general. The fact is, you can find almost everything, from tea bags to ready-made oven roast potatoes, all with less content in the packs than before. Why is it such a big deal for chocolate producers?

The difference is that people care hugely about their chocolate. A negative story on a highly sought-after and much-loved chocolate treat, with a following of terrified readers dreading a pending shortage of what they love, sells newspapers. Chocolate matters, and that's why it's been so topical.

Overall, the chocolate industry is not looking good today, especially I believe for some bigger players. It seems to have been hiding a lot of things, not by choice, admittedly. It's always easier to keep quiet, make cuts, and ignore the farmers. At least that's how it's been until recently, as many retailers and now consumers have forced the industry to be more transparent. Now many organizations and chocolate producers I know are working as hard as they can to change working conditions, save trees, and look after the planet, so things are improving. But you can only change so much. It's not an easy job reminding people what it is to be human again.

Things aren't necessarily improving for consumers, though. There isn't an organization that protects the size of your chocolate bar.

But again, many chocolate producers are stuck. Many don't have control over the prices charged by their suppliers. The producers don't make the chocolate (they just mold it), and the price of industrial ready-made chocolate has reportedly increased.

Did something I just said make you pause? Let me say it again just in case: *Many don't make their own chocolate.* Making chocolate on an industrial scale costs millions of dollars of investment. So instead, up to 65 percent of all chocolate producers buy chocolate from the big players, who supply it ready-made and offer it at a fixed price. Most chocolate is premade and arrives in tankers, warm from giant factories and delivered to what we imagine to be the chocolate factories. Alternatively, some producers will buy chocolate chips and heat them up. This premade chocolate is called "couverture," and it's supplied by just a few main global players, namely Barry Callebaut, Cargill, ADM,

Cémoi, and Petra Foods. There are others, but you get the idea. It's great chocolate, but it's a fact you should know.

Sorry to let you down. They mold it, adapt it, add to it, shape it, and pack it, but they don't make it. They make "chocolates," very different from making "chocolate."

Of course, this isn't true across the board. There are larger producers who have always made their own chocolate and subsequently maintained their unique taste. I can tell when I have a bar, but it's a subtle difference. This, I believe, is why there is such a successful wave of artisans and other producers that are going back to their roots and making their own tastes in chocolate by grinding and roasting their own beans. There are still many companies around today that make chocolate, but sadly not as many, I believe, as there used to be.

Say you are a producer and your ingredient prices have gone through the roof, you have to do something. What you do boils down to your priorities. Many of my friends are great chocolate producers and naturally they care a lot about their consumers (I hope some are still friends after they read this book!), but when I ask one or two of them, "What's your favorite chocolate?" they look me in the eye and say, "The one that makes the most money, Angus." Conversely, it's a diverse industry and I believe now at last that most producers want to focus on the planet, maintaining healthy consumers, and the farmers' ultimate well-being.

Chocolate products may continue to get smaller. Because of the demand for less sugar in our food products, new launches will provide evermore ingenious shapes and recipes to make something look like more chocolate than it is. As we choose to eat less sugar, the producers may choose to make products yet smaller in anticipation of being told by governments they are selling too much sugar per bar, a real and genuine challenge. We are being weaned onto smaller bars early before the potential sugar taxes come, which they already have in many places around the world.

Having said all that, everything in the end is in the taste and wanting it, right? I know people will always return to a great tasting product, like I do. I will often have a cup of coffee before bed (well, decaffeinated anyway) and have a dark Swiss chocolate, for example, but it's not only ever Swiss. I have chocolate from all over the world. It all tastes good, I surrender, I can't help it. *I like eating chocolate.*

No wait, I love it!

The mix of coffee and the cocoa bean is irresistible at 10:00 p.m. I succumb. I actually want one now as I write, especially after writing about chocolate all day and using up all these hard-earned brain calories. We use seventy calories an hour to just stay alive, do we need any more excuses? I have always claimed my biggest weaknesses are chocolate, champagne, and having more babies. My wife and I are the same—dangerous!

I am constantly considering how my food affects my personality and how my diet could better support this amazing planet that keeps me alive and better the person I am.

Somehow, I have to be a better person than I was yesterday. I can become a more responsible eater. Perhaps I have become totally obsessive, but I want to know what I eat. I read the small-print ingredients on the packets much more now and then go look them up and see what they might do to my body. I search alternative news sites about chemicals in what goes into my body (like fluoride in water) and reports from hushed scientists. Discovering the truth is powerful.

I can't change others, but I *can* change who I am and what I eat. I *can* cut down my sugar intake and therefore find that I enjoy the sweet moments more.

Above all, I try not to eat anything that is cruel to animals and people and avoid any product that destroys the beautiful trees and plants we cohabitate with. I have to honor the land and recognize the sacrifices that are made for me to eat and survive and allow for my freedom. My freedom is what allows me the choice to eat chocolate.

CHAPTER 16

Chocolate Just for the Moment

I now draw a close to the story of my not-so-extraordinary life of chaos and confectionery. The humble chocolate bar, those of us who eat it, and its impossibly sweet brothers and sisters are all changing for the better I feel. The industry is improving at last, but it has a long way to go. So do we in how much we need to know.

After all that's been said, chocolate is more than just plain sugar and fat. It's one of the few luxuries many of us can still afford after all our money is whisked away in bank charges, unfair fuel bills, nonsense speeding fines, crooked taxes and unfair laws, and mortgages on our already too-expensive properties that we could never afford anyway. Give a man a gun and he might rob a bank, but give a man a bank and he *will* rob the world. We live in a corrupt world that favors the constant delivery of unfair debit for the benefit of those in power, positioned like a pack of wolves to *almost* perfectly control us.

Our mission ultimately is to propagate what's left of our freedom. And perhaps our sweet and conveniently naughty-enough treats provide an escape during which we can break the rules a bit at a time when we know life is so disastrously restricting.

We know life is not right and a total bind, but chocolate provides us with a choice to have what we want for once and escape the endless torrent of no-can-do rules. Happiness is possessing a deep understanding of why it is that so many are sad, and making the choice to approach life with a different outlook.

If you can take a break, use it, enjoy what you eat (even if you choose a little less sugar), and seize your moment that is no one else's. Sit back and ignore the negativity that so many people offer, reject the lies, and cut through life's grand illusion. And there at last you might find your dream that has been waiting patiently for you all along.

Next time you retire into your favorite spot and bite into your treasured chocolate treat, above all, spare some time for yourself. Relax, tune out, and start the process of "unthinking," allowing the chocolate and relaxation to inspire you and fire up your true feelings. A unique time you have set aside for you, and you only.

For me this is what chocolate is all about. I can do what *I* want. I can seize my mind back when so many others require its attention.

So enjoy your treats and break away from the mold. Savor a unique time of no mobile phones, TV shows, pointless media fodder, piped music, polluted air, and random idiots talking incessantly without appearing to say anything meaningful. Grab a few minutes of peace during which you can finally and truly nourish your mind.

Whatever your dreams, chocolate-related or not, and wherever they lead you, I wish you the strength to follow them. It's my mission to help you. Never give up on a good (or God-given) thing, and stay positive no matter what is being thrown at you. It only takes one positive person to create another. I sincerely hope I have played a small part in this process for you, so make someone else feel good and take us all forward.

Hey, someone who chooses never to give up cannot ever be beaten.

In my life, I have never given up, even when things were really bad, and always, even in my darkest moments, I've believed that I could find freedom one day. I am still on that journey.

After many years of trying day after day, night after night, my dreams are coming true and at last the good prophecies made by the old bony-handed lady at number 22 in London really are happening. This is all wonderfully insane. In the end, being out of your mind is where sanity awaits.

And yet all I did was fail my way to success and allow for the tragedies. But all the time I hung on and ignored those people who said no when I wanted them to say yes and fought those who said "you can't" when I believed that I could. Rise above them and claim your freedom and ultimately your right to the happiness you so well deserve.

The next stage of my magnificent journey is to help you live your dreams. If you will allow me to continually serve you, that is.

I thank you with all my heart for joining me on this sweet and perhaps a little sour journey. But isn't that what makes a good life, learning from the lows and radiating our highs to those around us? My mission is our mission—we are all going to the same place in the end anyway, and I thank you for joining me on this quite unexpected occasion.

Remember you can always expect the unexpected, and that means wonderfully good things *will* happen for you, too. Please keep that thought as you put me down, and perhaps pick up a delish chocolate to take my place.

Keep it light and keep it sweet, and don't you ever give up on a good thing—you finally acting on those dreams. It's not about the path we take in life, but the baggage we choose to carry on the journey. God bless you and we'll be meeting again if you tune into my next stream of consciousness writing projects.

A Simple Way to Test the
Quality of Chocolate

I am often asked what the best chocolate is and where the best chocolates come from. The answer is entirely subjective. Many people like
very sweet, high sugar content, low cocoa butter content chocolate.
This is known in the industry as low-end, meaning the quality is not
as good and they're a lot cheaper to produce. Many people can't tell
the difference, whether their bar uses vegetable fat instead of expensive
cocoa butter. Well now I will show you how to know! It's actually very
easy to test your own chocolate at home with a few simple techniques.

This will work on any chocolate bar, light or dark. Dark chocolate
is not necessarily better quality. It just has more cocoa powder, the
element that gives its flavor—and that's a massive subject in itself!

- FIRST, CHECK THE APPEARANCE. Unwrap your chocolate bar
  and check to see if the surface of the bar is smooth and shiny
  with no bubble marks. Better quality bars tend to be shiny; it
  means they have been tempered better. A sludgy matte look is
  a sure sign that it has a high vegetable fat content.

- **Feel the texture.** A cheaper bar tends to have a rougher surface. Sometimes you'll find not-so-sharp edges of the molding. It doesn't change the taste, but it shows you that the molding machines and molds are due for replacement. This helps you build a picture of the care and attention taken in the production of your bar. Ideally, the edges should be sharp and clearly defined.

- **Look for blooming.** Sometimes you will see a chocolate bar with a kind of white area on it. This is called blooming and can often be unfairly blamed on the chocolate producer. It is not linked to bad quality, but it does show that the storekeeper allowed your chocolate bar to melt and re-set. This is not the fault of the producer, but they would be really pleased if you let them know so they can track its transit to your local shop.

- **Make sure the chocolate is room temperature.** There's no sense in doing the following snap test if the chocolate is too cold. If it's too warm, you can cool it in the refrigerator for a better result.

- **Break a piece off.** Okay, most people by now have probably given up waiting to taste their chocolate. Those of you who have exercised your self-control may now break off a piece of the bar. Listen to it snap. If it clicks, it's high quality. Pay attention; it's kind of a high-pitched click. (This will vary a little depending on how thick the bar is.) A bar with very low cocoa butter content (low quality) may not snap at all; some even bend before they break. But the high-quality bar will snap with a clean break, thanks to the higher amount of crystalized cocoa butter.

ACKNOWLEDGMENTS

Thank you to my late mum and dad for bringing me into the world—oh, and their parents for bringing them in, too. But wait . . . I had better thank *their* parents as well, can't leave them out. Where do I stop?

And what's the point of thanking anyone when I wouldn't exist without a few essential items, such as Mother Earth, the planets, the bees, and all my fellow creatures that live on this planet? And I definitely can't leave out our dear kitten, now called Cocoa, whom I found in a ditch in the garden and rescued from death after a fox attack.

Yes, I thank all of existence, my gods, the unseen spirits, the universal energy, and my ancient alien friends—the Arcturians and the ever-so-cool Pleiadians—and cheers to the ultimate creator of love. Nice job, mate.

If it weren't for Julia Abramoff, the tireless and dedicated publisher at Apollo who spotted me and pulled me out of the chocolate world, recognizing the *"great intention,"* there would be no book at all. I wouldn't even be able to give any thanks. How bad is that! But hey, Julia and Alex Merrill at Apollo Publishers are living the dream magnificently, and my hat goes off to them for creating a wonderful publishing house that's set to go places. I can't wait to read all their amazing books.

Previous to working with Apollo, I edited seven of my own titles. What a refreshing experience to have an eagle-eyed and quick-witted editor like Tiffany Hill to bounce ideas off and fine-tune this work. Thanks, Tiff—let's do it again; you made me laugh so much. Priceless.

There are many others in the book industry who go unrecognized: the book buyers, proofreaders, editors, retailers, producers, and promoters, even the fork-lift drivers who will have to load up thousands of copies of my book!

This is going to fly, we know, so thank you all for keeping the book trade alive and kicking, hopefully even more when you get stuck in *Bittersweet*. Cheers to all my friends in the chocolate industry too. I trust you will still be my friends after you've read this book! You are all wonderful people doing a good thing providing for our sweetest pleasures. We need pleasure now more than ever.

The other night, my wife, Sophie, and I went for a meal at our magnificent local curry house on London Road in Maidstone, UK. My wife had just, after many years, reread one of the books I wrote. She was welling up with tears and said, "It was a truly beautiful book. Don't you ever give up, Angus." Blimey, she got me reaching for the pressed linen napkins, wiping my eyes over a papadum, and snivelling too! Thank you, Sophie, for putting up with me and my incurable but rather magnificent malady, the never-ever-giving-up-on-living-the-dream syndrome. Yes, Sophie, for being there time after time for me when I was knocked down on so many thousands of occasions. You were with me through decades of rejections and false promises. But look now: we absolutely smashed it.

Leon, my eldest son, you always pulled me up when I was down. You even listened with a philosophical ear to the earlier chapters late at night when even our sausage dog would not listen to me and started running out of the lounge the moment I read out loud. Amazing Leon.

Lorna, my eldest daughter, thank you for throwing the greatest and most hideously monstrous teenage parties at our house and bringing me back to my youth with your smile and your amazing friends and persona. You keep me alive, inspired, in touch with youth, and with it—the real new world and ultimately what we want to read.

And then Ruby. (Yes, I am going through all the kids!) Thank you for your outrageous art and for making me laugh when I so needed to. I mean, superimposing my face on the head of a sausage dog for our Christmas board games? Truly unsurpassable. Oh, and for reminding me that your friends keep asking when my next book is coming! Well here it is, folks; hooray all around. I needed that, Ruby. Writers (I am sure many are reading this) can write for decades, never knowing if it will ever happen. Stick at it, okay? It can.

And George, the quiet thinker. I sat on your bed late at night when we all should have been asleep, reading *Bittersweet* in its early stages— and you didn't even mind when I rewrote it and reread it again. You are wise counsel, George, an old soul. We had some fun, right? Let's do that again with secret hazelnut truffles at midnight next time.

And finally, Kieran, my youngest son, thank you for making it utterly impossible to write anything with any meaning at all, ever. You smashed it. Charging round the house chasing the dog, throwing Lego helicopters across the room, terrorizing the cat, and generally teaching us all that life goes on outside of the mundane distractions of iPhones and tablets, no matter what. Kieran, if it weren't for you, I would never have written *The Kitchen Baby*, the book that made Mum laugh and cry over a curry, and now another best seller. Thanks, son. One day you should read it and this message too, okay?

There are many people I have been in touch with over the years who I have bored to death about my writing energies. I thank you all for just listening to my impossible dreams that at times, even Angus Kennedy nearly gave up, so thanks for inspiring me to keep going. My dreams are now finally coming to life. I share this energy of pleasure with you.

And finally, there is, of course, you. I don't know you, but I *feel* who you are already. I thank you for taking the plunge into the magical life of confections and reading a story of chocolates, magic, and surviving the impossible. Life is such a ride. It's your energy and good thoughts that sculpt people like me into writers.

The rest is up to you. Not me. You know that. I thank you for joining me on this amazing journey. If you allow me to continue, then, man, there is a whole ton more to come. Stay tuned, be strong, and don't give up on a good thing, because you know what? It's never going to give up on you. Believe it, and it's coming.

22 Metheun Park, the house where I grew up.

2

Photograph of
wife

RUSWELL HILL

LONDON N.10

Signature of bearer
Signature du titulaire Angus Kenn

Signature of wife
Signature de sa femme

WARNING TO HOLDER

d with this passpor

My childhood passport. I'm ten in the photo.

Mum, circa 1980.

My dad, John Kennedy.

My wife, Sophie, and our son Keiran, one of our five amazing
children.

Me and Boyd Tunnock, CEO of Tunnock's, in the Tunnock's factory.
Boyd has always inspired me.

Angus Kennedy, the face of chocolate.

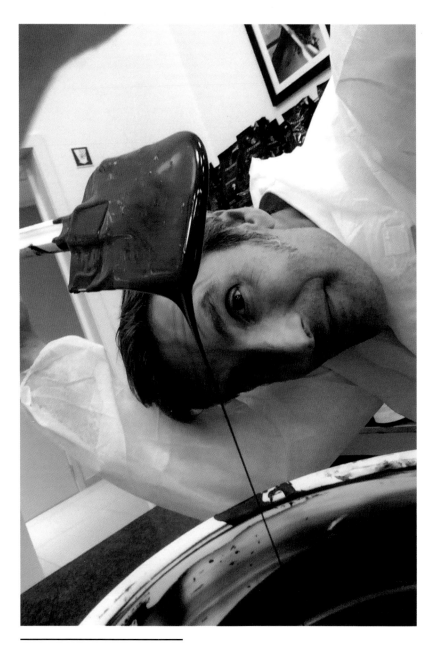

Me assessing the quality of some wonderful chocolate.